INFINITE BASEBALL

INFINITE BASEBALL

Notes from a Philosopher at the Ballpark

Alva Noë

OXFORD
UNIVERSITY PRESS

Oxford University Press is a department of the University of Oxford. It furthers
the University's objective of excellence in research, scholarship, and education
by publishing worldwide. Oxford is a registered trade mark of Oxford University
Press in the UK and certain other countries.

Published in the United States of America by Oxford University Press
198 Madison Avenue, New York, NY 10016, United States of America.

CIP data is on file at the Library of Congress
ISBN 978-0-19-092818-6

Printed by Sheridan Books, Inc., United States of America

For Ulysses

The goal is to arrive at immediacy *after* reflection.

—KIERKEGAARD

CONTENTS

Preface xiii

The Infinite Game 1

In Praise of Being Bored

1. Do We Need to Speed Up Baseball? 31

2. In Praise of Being Bored 36

3. Three Cheers for Instant Replay 39

4. The Problem with Baseball on TV 42

5. Joint Attention 45

Keeping Score

6. The Forensic Sport 51

7. No-Hitters, Perfect Games, and the Meaning of Life 54

8. Keeping Score 59

9. The Numbers Game 63

The Communication Game

10. Baseball and the Nature of Language 71

11. Linguistic Universals 79

12. The Communication Game 85

13. A Moment Misunderstood 89

14. Nobody's Perfect 93

Making Peace With Our Cyborg Nature

15. "The Positive Role of Medicine in Our Game's Growth" 99

16. Making Peace with Our Cyborg Nature 105

17. Plagiarized Performance 108

18. What Can a Person Do? 115

19. In Defense of Barry Bonds 120

20. Legalize It! 123

21. How Much Baseball Is Too Much? 128

22. The Athlete and the Gladiator 134

Baseball Memories

23. Heartbreak and Social Media 139

24. The Matt Harvey Affair 144

25. Explaining the Magic of the Ballpark 149

26. For the Love of the Game: Play Ball! 152

27. How to Be a Fan 155

28. Mind over Matter 159

29. Reflections on the "Boys" of Summer 163

30. Baseball's Great Equalizer 165

31. Beep Baseball 167

32. Baseball Memories 170

ACKNOWLEDGMENTS 175
BIBLIOGRAPHY 181
INDEX 185

PREFACE

This is a book about baseball. Or, rather, it's a book about base-ball by a philosopher. But do not be alarmed. It is not a work of philosophy, at least not in the conventional, academic sense. Most of the short writings gathered here were published between 2010 and 2017 on National Public Radio's now sadly defunct science and culture website *13.7: Cosmos and Culture*. Many of them were occasioned by current events; all of them were meant to be standalone pieces of writing. Because—as I soon came to realize— they work together to articulate a new idea about baseball and its broader significance, I decided to publish them together in single volume.

The introductory chapter is a different animal. I have written it, in good measure, to try to integrate and organize the ideas contained in the short chapters that follow. It is a work of phi-losophy, although again I would say not of the conventional aca-demic variety. Its purpose is to defend the following claims about baseball, all of which are explored, with a somewhat lighter touch, in the chapters themselves:

- What happens in baseball is less a matter of the material facts on the ground than it is a matter of who did what—that is, who is to be credited with this or that action. To play baseball is always to be absorbed in the task of figuring out how to apportion praise and blame. Baseball's concerns are, in this sense, forensic or juridical.

- The activity of playing the game contains the activity of this reflection on itself as a part. In this respect, it is like the law, and like language.

- Scorekeeping in baseball is not something we do from the outside, as it were, looking in. *Figuring out the score*, making up the account, telling the story—this is one of baseball's essential activities.

- It is widely believed that baseball is a numbers game. But it isn't. Not really. It's not a quantitative game. It's a normative game, for its main concern is *who deserves credit or blame for what*. In this sense, it is a philosophical game.

I discuss a wide range of other topics in the short writings collected here, ranging from the nature of fandom and the baseball-like character of language, to the use of so-called performance-enhancing drugs, to the charms and values of youth baseball. The reader is invited to dip in without preparation; this is not a book that needs to be read from start to finish. I hope the essays stimulate and give pleasure.

INFINITE BASEBALL

THE INFINITE GAME
AN INTRODUCTION

Pitcher
His art is eccentricity, his aim
How not to hit the mark he seems to aim at,

His passion how to avoid the obvious,
His technique how to vary the avoidance.

The others throw to be comprehended. He
Throws to be a moment misunderstood.

Yet not too much. Not errant, arrant, wild,
But every seeming aberration willed.

Not to, yet still, still to communicate
Making the batter understand too late.

—ROBERT FRANCIS

Plato said that the gods love what is good; things are not good because the gods love them.

It's the other way around when it comes to baseball. It's just a game, but we make it good through our love. We don't play baseball and watch it and write about it and think about it because it is so darn special. It's special—it *is* special—because we care so much about it, because we play baseball and sing its praises and write about it and endeavor to revise it and make it better.

1

Stop and watch the kids playing baseball at the local field. Take a good look. Now ask yourself, What are they doing? You see them pitch, hit, run, throw, catch. You see them make plays. *Man on first, one out, hard grounder to short; No outs, runners on first and third, ball popped up to the pitcher.* But you also see them talk. There is a lot of talking. What are they talking about? They're telling each other what to do, they are explaining what they did wrong; they are jabbering to distract, but also to motivate; they're thinking about what the next pitch should be, or what it's likely to be. They're directing each other, signaling back and forth, attempting in real time to get a handle on the situation. They talk as they practice and play, and their talk concerns the stuff, all that matters, of their activity. They listen. They try to focus. They also sit, stretch, swing bats, study playbooks, put on masks and chest protectors, adjust cups; they eat, drink, spit, laugh, curse. They chant and they call out: "Good eye! Good eye!" or "You got this!" or "Two strikes now. Gotta protect! Gotta protect!" They cast glances at their parents. They work hard to manage their emotions.

And the boys and girls on the field are not alone in this free-wheeling conversation and engagement with the play. The coaches are in the thick of it. As are the umps, if there are any. And then there are the spectators. They are no less invested in the actions that do not so much unfold before them as lure them in and make them complicit. They don't just watch; they cheer; they command and advise; they participate in the practice of trying, in effect, to articulate, or of trying to grasp and keep track of, the game. They scatter when a ball is hit into foul territory to make room so the fielders can play the ball.

Where does the game stop and all this chatter and observation and debate begin? If you look and pay attention, you'll have to admit, the limits of the game are not drawn, in any straightforward sense, around the field of play itself. Baseball, in truth, is a practice that is bigger than that.

There is so much writing about baseball, not just good writing, but good writing by intellectuals. No other American sport, with the possible exception of boxing, as others have noticed, has come close to attracting the attention not only of fans and specialists but also of intellectuals who feel called on not just to celebrate the game but also to understand it, and to find the words to say why we love it so. Stephen Jay Gould, the great paleontologist and scholar of evolutionary history, took up this question in the introduction to his own collected writings on baseball. (Yes, he wrote a collection of writings on baseball.[1]) *Why?* Why so much intellectual focus on baseball? Is the game different from other games? Is it just that hard, or complex, or mathematical? Or might it be, as Gould also considered, that it is because baseball so perfectly, and so uniquely, imitates life—its circular, seasonal rhythms, its meanings (trying to be "safe" and get "home")—that baseball alone among games and sports is a fitting stand-in for reflection on the more lofty theme of life itself?

Gould took a tentative stab at a negative answer. Baseball is the national pastime, he assumed—that is, it is the dominant game in

---

1. Stephen Jay Gould, *Triumph and Tragedy in Mudville: A Lifelong Passion for Baseball* (New York: Norton, 2003). There is too much good baseball writing to offer anything like a complete list here, but I'll mention these personal favorites: in addition to Gould's writings, Chad Harbach's novel, *The Art of Fielding*; John Updike's essay on Ted Williams, "Hub Fans Bid Kid Adieu"; George F. Will's *Men at Work: The Craft of Baseball* (New York: Macmillan, 1990); and everything by Roger Angell.

the gaming ecosystem. If there's more intellectual writing about baseball, he reasoned, then this is because there happen to be more baseball fans and not because a higher percentage of baseball fans, as compared to fans of other sports, are intellectual, or because baseball, on the intrinsic merits, demands more of the intellect.[2]

Gould was on to something; he nailed the blunt contingency of our love of the game. We grow up to love the foods we grow up eating, and we find it easiest to give full expression to our thoughts and feelings in the language we grow up speaking. And so with baseball and other sports. We love—and experience most fully the virtues of—the games we grow up playing. And those of us who are "intellectuals" express that love in the form of serious writing. To suppose that there's something about the game itself that makes it especially worthy of thought and attention smacks of the sort of chauvinism that might lead someone to think that his homely cuisine, or his mother tongue, is somehow, truly, superior.

In this book I suggest a more radical explanation of baseball's link to writing: baseball, from the very first, is a thinking game, a game that demands of its players that they seek, in their role as players, to fathom and articulate the game. If I am right, then thoughtful writing on baseball of the sort that Gould produced— and that I am trying to produce—*is* baseball. Baseball includes all

---

2. Is baseball as popular today as it once was? Is it still the dominant game in the gaming ecosystem? Maybe not. But it remains the case that there's more writing about baseball than other sports. I conducted an unscientific survey, with the help of Google Books. It would appear that there have been more books published on baseball in the last twenty years—hundreds more—than about football (both American football *and* soccer).

that. It comprehends the ways we use baseball to understand both what is and what is not baseball.

This idea—that baseball is a kind of reflective activity—is a philosophical one. Baseball, in this sense, is a philosophical game.

When I say that baseball is a thinking game, I don't mean that its performance is primarily intellectual, or that baseball players are philosophers. The philosopher Jerrold Levinson once remarked, in response to hearing me talk about this, that while growing up in Brooklyn, he knew some pretty strong baseball players, but he wouldn't have been inclined to say that their excellence corresponded to wit or brain power. He offered this as an objection to the idea that baseball is reflective in the way I am suggesting.

So let me clarify. It is not my claim that baseball is an intellectual undertaking like philosophy. That would be silly. That's no more true than the claim that to know a language you need to be a linguist, or that to be a cop you've got to be a lawyer. If you've spent time around the game, you know that isn't true. Sure, there are some deep-thinking, smart baseball players, but the clubhouse is not a place where you can expect to hear a lot of intellectually elevated talk.

And yet we need to tread carefully here. If you speak a language, then you've probably had occasion to think about language use. For example, you've probably wondered whether you are using a word correctly. Or noticed or been puzzled by the word usage of another person. Maybe you've explained a word's meaning to a kid, or felt critical of someone because he or she was hard to follow— that is, hard to understand. It would be crazy to say that to be a speaker you need to be a scholar of language. But it is a deep and, I think, often overlooked fact about language that to know a language, you need to be sensitive to the kinds of problems that language use itself presents.[3]

And the same is true with baseball. There's no playing it without participating thoughtfully in the problems it raises. Nothing brings this out more than the preoccupation, *inside* baseball, with keeping score. Scorekeeping in baseball isn't just a matter of knowing the score. It is, at once, an analytic activity of figuring out what happened and a graphical practice of applying, or devising, notations for the purpose of writing it all down. We aim, when keeping score, to figure out *how* to score the play (e.g., we score the runner's out at the plate 7–6–2—that is, the leftfielder relayed the ball to the cut-off shortstop, who threw to the catcher, who made the tag at the plate). Scoring requires knowledge and it requires judgment. It

---

3. I have written about this in my book *Strange Tools: Art and Human Nature* (New York: Farrar, Straus and Giroux, 2015), and also in an essay called "The Writerly Attitude" (in *Symbolic Articulation: Image, Word, and Body Between Action and Schema*, edited by Sabine Marienberg; Berlin, Boston: Walter de Gruyter, 2017), and I discuss it further in chapters 10 and 11 of this book. Commenting on a version of "The Writerly Attitude," the philosopher Barry Stroud said, very much in the spirit of Levinson's remark mentioned above, that I'm giving language users too much credit. There are a lot of people out there whose speech is more or less confined to a practiced grunting. That is exactly what I'm denying. We too easily overlook the immense conceptual and rhetorical complexity of even our most simple communication situations. This was a point the philosopher Wittgenstein has made, and it is also one that has more recently become the subject of new work in linguistics on the ubiquity in languages of words for linguistic *repair*—that is, clarification, disambiguation, and so on. On this, see Nick Enfield's *How We Talk: The Inner Workings of Conversation* (New York: Basic Books, 2017), as well as chapter 11, in which Enfield's ideas are discussed.

requires making decisions about, for example, whether a bunt up the third-base line is a failed attempt to get on base or whether, rather, it is a sacrifice; if we say the latter, then we don't even count the batter's actions at the plate as an at-bat; we appreciate that he *sacrificed* his at-bat, his chance to get a hit, in order to advance the runner; or about whether the second baseman committed an error in failing to play the ground ball, or whether it was a hit, pure and simple; when we say it was a hit, we mean that we can't blame the fielder for having missed it. And there are questions such as whether runs scored on a pitcher should be counted as *earned runs*, or whether they are the result of fielding errors beyond the pitcher's control. Keeping score, then, is at once an intimate look not just at what happened but also at how what happened is really a matter of sourcing praise and blame and interpreting the significance of what's going on. Baseball reality is fixed less by what happens than by the question of who's responsible for what happens. And it is *forensic* matters such as these that are the main preoccupation of the baseball scorekeeper.[4] And crucially, scorekeeping isn't

---

4. John Locke called *person* a forensic concept. What he had in mind is that a person is one to whom credit and blame may be attached, one who is deemed responsible. The concept of a person is the concept of an *agent*. Crucially, Locke argued, persons are not the same as human beings. Dr. Jekyll and Mr. Hyde may be one and the same *human being*—that is, one and the same continuously existing organic life; they share a birth event; but they are, or may be, two distinct *persons*. And this is why we may feel that it would be unfair to blame the one for the other's crimes. Multiple personality disorder is perhaps a real-world example of this. Some readers probably associate *forensic* with TV crime procedurals and the use of the science of fingerprints and DNA to catch criminals. I am using it here in Locke's sense, which is closely related to this more familiar meaning. The objective of the forensic scientist, after all, is to figure out who is responsible for the crime.

something that takes place outside the game, a mere matter of *recording,* like, for example, the activity of filming a game for broadcast. It belongs to the game's play. It is a thoughtful activity that is essential to the game, to its unfolding dynamics and rationale. And the scorekeeper's perspective—if not the actual task of writing it all down—is the perspective taken up, it is the perspective that *needs to be taken up,* by the players themselves. To play the game is to be interested in the score, and to be concerned with the basic challenges posed by the task of accurate scorekeeping.

Baseball is an infinite game.[5]

Or to make the point differently, it isn't really a game at all; it is a world. Let me explain.

Finite games are fixed, fixed in space and time, and fixed by the rules. They are well defined. They don't just start and stop; they have beginnings and are brought to a conclusion; their evolution is regulated and definite. Finite games have a goal, or an end, and it is always determinate, or at least agreed upon, when these have been met. You play to win, to score, and so on.

Finite games are mechanical and so, in principle at least, we can build mechanisms to mimic their play. It is because, or to the degree that, chess is a finite game that we can simulate chess play with computers.[6]

---

5. The idea of finite versus infinite games is due to James P. Carse. See his *Finite and Infinite Games: A Vision of Life as Play and Possibility* (New York: Free Press, 1986). Thanks to William Forsythe for introducing me to Carse's writing.

6. I write here of the "simulation of chess play" because I have never been persuaded that computers *play* anything, let alone chess. This may have to do with the fact that when it comes to computers, we cannot speak of an appreciation of the infinite (in the sense used in the text).

Baseball isn't mechanical in this way, just as life itself is not mechanical. Baseball isn't finite. It is much more human than that.

There are pitching machines, and there's nothing far-fetched about machines that run, field, or hit. But baseball isn't pitching, running, fielding, or hitting.

Baseball isn't just an activity, made up of subactivities. It is a domain of play; it is a field of thought; it is, as I put it, a practice. To play baseball is not just to run, catch, hit, and throw. It is to live in the baseball world. To play baseball you must care about baseball, have a stake in it, think about it. (No machine does that.)

With some activities we can distinguish the activity from thought about the activity. We can distinguish, as it were, theory and practice. But some activities contain, as modes of themselves, theory. Some activities, the ones I call practices, always require reflection.

Baseball is one of these. To play baseball is to engage with the problem of baseball. Baseball is a problem to itself.

It is a cliché that baseball is a microcosm of life itself. But this is just because baseball is a social world and so it exhibits the structural properties of social worlds. The thing about social worlds is that they are not fixed or stable or governed, once and for all, by rules. Social life is a field in which the rules are themselves, explicitly or implicitly, contested.

But aren't the rules of baseball, like the rules of chess, fixed? Isn't a baseball game the most definite thing there is? Isn't it possible, when it comes to baseball, to make everything explicit?

Baseball isn't the men on the diamond doing what they do. Baseball is also the practice of trying to understand what the men on the diamond are doing not only while they are doing it but also in the larger setting of the game's past and future. It is something that engages not only the coaches and managers and trainers but also the players and umpires and fans. Take away the *reflection on* and you are left with mere activity—with something robots could do. And that's not baseball. Baseball without umps and coaches and fans and players trying to decide what's happening on the field of play would no more be baseball than justice would be at work in a courtroom in which there were no parties to dispute vying with each other to resolve their conflict.

And while this game or that, and while the playing season as a whole, may come to an end, the practice of baseball, the baseball world, cannot end in this way.

Which is not to say that we cannot leave it, or give it up, or even destroy it.

The baseball world is our world.

My claim is that baseball is an infinite game; this means that it can't be divided into first-order play and second-order theory about the play. The game contains its own theory of itself; it is meta from the start. Baseball is a practice, not a mere activity. Its rules are its subject matter as much as they are its definition. Baseball is a field.

Now, it is not my point that baseball is unique in exhibiting this looped reflective structure. Actually, my point is just the opposite. It is the hallmark of all characteristically human activities—language, the law, other sports—that they are, in the sense I am trying to understand, *baseball-like*. Human practices of this kind can't be reduced to mere activities. Or, rather, the activities themselves comprehend the work of rethinking and so remaking the activity itself. Human cultural life is made up of open-textured reflective activities; human cultural life is enacted through doing and reflecting on what one does. Human life is, in this sense, baseball-like.

There is a widespread idea—I'll call it the myth of flow—according to which skillfulness, expertise, and, indeed, wisdom find their fullest expression when we are *in the zone*, when we are carried away, in the flow. The shortstop or the saxophonist or the dancer or the fighter achieves mastery when he or she goes beyond rationality, choice, and agency, and enters a zone of automaticity and attunement that is beyond all that. The wise person, whom Aristotle called the *phronesis,* is not brainy, not a careful deliberator, but, rather, one who is able intuitively to discern the right course of action. We are at our truly human best, according to the myth of flow, when we operate in a mode of engaged selflessness. We are unactualized, so the myth would have it, when we are thoughtful, detached, and deliberate.

Baseball, I urge in this book, is not an activity that admits of this kind of nondeliberative, selfless commitment. It doesn't have the right kind of structure. We don't lose ourselves in baseball; there is, in a way, nothing to lose ourselves in. There is nothing that flows. Nothing for us to get lost in. True, as we have noticed already, there may be flow at the level of individual plays. But baseball as a whole is a domain whose interests and values and problems need to be worked out, coped with, in real time, by the players.

Baseball doesn't lend itself to the flow state; it doesn't have the right structure. But this is because the same is true of human life more generally. Life isn't mindless flow punctuated by episodes of breakdown in which it is necessary to stop and think. Wit and intelligence are not detached from skillful action in this way. Indeed, what makes the skillful shortstop, or the saxophone player, remarkable is not that he or she can play without thinking but, instead, that the thinking unfolds actively in the playing.

The myth of flow is just that: a myth. And it is wrong not only because of the false image of engagement—being in the zone—that it promulgates but also because of the false, hyper-intellectual picture of rationality to which the flow state is opposed.

Life is much more baseball-like than that. Life is a delicate balance of action and thought, immediacy and reflection, of the achievement of immediacy in and through reflection. Or, as Dewey would have put it, we do and we undergo and we keep track of the relation between our doing and our undergoing; it is in this, in our knowing active engagement, that our intelligence is expressed.

And so, far from insisting that baseball is unique among sports or games in its demand that reflective engagement with the play is part of the playing itself, I wish to insist that this could not be the case. For this reflective looping structure belongs to all human practices.

But I do want to suggest that baseball thematizes just this fact about itself, and about its own performance, more directly and more experimentally, than most other sports—cricket perhaps being an exception—or indeed, most other domains of human practice. This comes out in the fact that baseball, as I argue in this book, is so thoroughly obsessed with, as I put it, forensic matters—with questions about who deserves credit or blame for what happens on the field—and also in the fact that baseball is remarkably focused not just on storytelling but also on finding ways to *write the story down*, very literally, on the scorecard. Baseball is, in this sense, historical and history making.

A comparison with boxing may be helpful. Boxing, too, exhibits a richly normative forensic structure—that is to say, its action depends not just on what happened but also on our evaluation of who gets credited or blamed for what happened, and so on the stories we tell about the fight. The fighter falls; but was it the effectiveness of his opponent's strike that sent him to the mat, or did he slip? This matters for how the round gets scored and can be decisive in determining the bout's outcome. In boxing it sometimes happens that matches are decided by "split decision"—that is, the judges may disagree in their assignment of points. This builds into the method of scoring the fact that the score can't be settled by algorithm, that it depends on the always interpretive question of who gets credit for having done what. The mere fact of what happened—punch is thrown, fighter goes down—leaves the question what really happened unanswered. To tell the story of the bout, to give a proper account, is to fill in these forensic matters.

But it is in baseball, not boxing, that the players themselves, in their role as players, as well as the knowledgeable spectator, are concerned throughout adequately to write the game down, on paper, literally, as it unfolds. The forensic, normative structure at play is not unique to baseball, but baseball's explicit engagement with the problem of scorekeeping is a distinguishing feature of the sport.[7]

Baseball is distinctly engaged with the problem of telling its own story, with finding the right way to write itself down. A musical score is forward looking; it is a tool for making music. A baseball score is backward looking; it is a tool for making sense of what is already under way.

From earliest days, baseball folk hit on the use of numbers as a satisfying and tidy way to tell the story of the game. Because baseball is, or at least seems to be, a game of discrete events whose significance depends on the way these numbers pile up, counting events and other achievements and keeping track of their frequency have proved indispensable to the production of baseball narrative.

This is strikingly in evidence in the box score, a little 1-inch numerical grid that gives you a summary of the game, an abstract of the action. It used to be that newspapers would publish all the day's box scores, spread out across one or two pages, and often

---

7. Perhaps what explains the fact, noticed already, that there is also a fair bit of intellectual writing about boxing is precisely the fact that the impulse to make what has happened explicit, to understand it and write it down, is at work in boxing in something like the way it is at work in baseball. When it comes to baseball and boxing, there is a story that needs working out. Joyce Carol Oates writes: "Each boxing match is a story—a unique and highly condensed drama without words. Even when nothing sensational happens; then the drama is '"merely"' psychological. Boxers are there to establish an absolute experience, a public accounting of the outmost limits of their beings" (Oates 1987, 8). And she says: "Because a boxing match is a story without words, this doesn't mean that it has no text or no language, that it is somehow '"brute,"' '"primitive,"' '"inarticulate,"' only that the text is improvised in action. . . . [B]oxing as performance is more clearly akin to dancing or music than narrative" (11).

accompanied by lists of other statistics such as team or league leaders in batting average, home runs, runs batted in, or the familiar pitching categories of wins, earned run average, strikeouts and saves. In addition to all this, of course, newspapers would run, and still run, the all-important *standings*—that is, the rankings of teams, in divisions and leagues, by their winning percentage (the ratio of their wins to losses). Who wins the division and makes it into the postseason, in baseball, comes down to the math.

It should come as no surprise that the correct use of numbers has been, from earliest days, a source of controversy in the baseball world. It wouldn't be an exaggeration to say that the game's history is the history of evolving ways of making use of statistics to measure achievement and evaluate performance.

For example, how do you sum up a pitcher's performance in a few numbers? As Alan Schwarz recounts in *The Numbers Game*, it was only in 1912, and after years of passionate resistance, that baseball statistician John Heydler succeeded in pushing through earned run average (ERA), the average of earned runs per nine-inning game, as a settled measure of overall pitching effectiveness. What made ERA controversial, then, and even today, is the problem of getting clear on what is to count as an earned run. For example, does a run that scores because of a stolen base count as earned—that is, do we think that the pitcher should be held responsible for giving it up? Or consider this: we don't hold a pitcher responsible for anything that happens after an error on what would have been the third out; the logic is clear—but for the bungling of a fielder, the inning would have been over; so you can't blame *the pitcher* for anything that happens after that. But suppose that with two outs and an inning extended by error a pitcher gives up three consecutive hits followed by a grand-slam home run. On what planet is it reasonable to think that none of that reflects on the quality of the pitcher's performance? It is for these reasons that statisticians and others bent on using the numbers to lay bare the elements of the game seek to identify a way of measuring a pitcher's quality of performance that is independent of the factors over which the pitcher has no control (e.g., the quality of his own team's defense, the vicissitudes of the venue or the weather, etc.).

Over the last few decades we have witnessed a revolution in what is now called "baseball analytics." This story is told in Michael Lewis's book *Moneyball* (and later in the film of the same name): Oakland A's general manager Billy Beane drew on new math and novel models to identify and tap into hitherto undiscovered and underappreciated veins of talent. To give an example, the new baseball analytics looks askance at batting average—surely one of the most popular, intuitive, and well-entrenched statistics; to be the league leader in batting average is *to be* the Batting Champion—on the grounds that batting average fails to take into account the fact that hits aren't the only way to get on base and that, crucially, not all hits are equal in value (e.g., home runs are worth more than singles). The new "quants" prefer, in place of batting average, measures such as on-base percentage (the rate at which a hitter gets on base, by whatever means, walks, hits, hit-by-pitches, etc.) and slugging percentage (the number of *bases* per at-bat). From the standpoint of these statistics it is possible to appreciate that sometimes low-status hitters, by traditional lights—low average, lots of strikeouts—may in fact be of greater value to a team's prospects than hitters who hit for high average.

Or consider such hallowed marks of baseball accomplishment as pitcher's wins and batter's runs batted in (RBIs). According to the new analytics, these statistics are false idols that have misled not only generations of fans but also generations of managers, general managers, and players. Pitchers don't win games, *teams* do. You can pitch well and not win, or pitch poorly and get the win. Why treat a measure outside the control of the pitcher as a measure of his quality and accomplishment? And it's the same with RBIs: you can only knock runs in if there are already runners on base. You could bat 1.000 and still have no RBIs, if no one ahead of you in the line-up ever reaches base (and if you hit no home runs).

Whether you are persuaded by these considerations to abandon all thought of wins and RBIs, it is impossible to fail to be impressed with the way new numbers-based analysis, buoyed by the ubiquitous and ready availability of new technologies of big data, is changing the game. It is now possible, as it was never before, to model a player's performance at the most fine-grained levels of resolution. If you need to know how a righty batter performs against two-strike fastballs, low and inside, delivered by southpaws, on Thursday nights, in the Eastern Time Zone, playing after a day of rest, you can probably find out with just a few clicks, at least in principle.

Anyone who's ever played in the outfield knows how important it is to have some advance knowledge of where the batter is likely to hit the ball. Should you play a batter deep, or shallow, on the line or away from it? This knowledge can make the difference between routine outs and acrobatic plays, or failing to get an out at all. It is now routine for teams "to put on the shift"—that is, radically to realign the position of defensive players based on statistically well-grounded models of where a given batter likes to hit. In the absence of reliable information about where batters are likely to hit, it makes good sense to position players around the field to cover as much ground as possible. That's the logic behind the traditional assignment of defensive players to "positions" around the diamond. But there's no need to cover the whole field if you can know, in advance, that certain batters will systematically favor or neglect different zones. If the hitter's job is to "hit it where they ain't," then the fielder's job is to put himself where they're gonna hit it, and that's something it is now possible to do with a surprisingly high degree of success.

Baseball players, like everyone else, it turns out, act within an arc inscribed by habit. And habit can be described with numbers.

For all these reasons—because of the enduring importance of statistical analysis in our understanding of baseball—it is reasonable to say, as many do, that baseball is a numbers game. The numbers contribute hugely, and always have done, to our understanding of performance. But the idea that baseball is a numbers game can be, and I think has frequently tended to be, misleading. The numbers are important precisely because we use them to think about and tell the story of the game. But the story isn't a story about numbers. Numbers are not, and cannot be, a substitute for the kind of interpretation and evaluation—figuring out what's going on and why it matters, making sense of who is doing what now and of who can be expected to perform well in the future— that is what is truly at stake in baseball (as in life). Numbers are subordinate to the all-important problem of understanding the game and telling its story.

The idea that baseball somehow bottoms out in quantitative analysis is a huge mistake. Remarkably, its distorting influence is almost ubiquitous in the baseball world.

Consider conventional wisdom about the pitcher–batter showdown. On the standard story, it's all about man against physics or, rather, man against the limits of human physiology. The baseball, we are reminded, is thrown *too fast* for a batter even really to see it, let alone have time to make a decision about how or where to swing. So the hitter is required to work in the space of impossibility.[8] The pitcher, for his part, is a speed machine; and the history of the pitching game, from Walter Johnson down through Sandy Koufax and Nolan Ryan, to the present day, is assumed to be the history of the ever more powerful fastball.[9] Pitchers strive for power-based dominance by any means necessary; they push their bodies beyond all reasonable natural limits, and the price they pay, quite literally, is pain and suffering. Surgical repair of pitchers' arms is almost normal these days, not to say epidemic, and soaking the arm in a bucket of ice after a game is something even Little Leaguers learn to do by the time they're twelve. Nothing

---

8. As Zack Schonbrun, writing in the *New York Times*, puts it: "The resulting time we have to actually gauge the pitch is almost twice as fast as an eye blink. It is slightly slower than the duration of one rotation of a helicopter rotor blade. But in the time it takes to read this word, the ball will have sailed past. It should not seem a wonder, then, that it has been more than 75 years since an M.L.B. player batted .400. It should seem a wonder that our brains enable us to ever hit the ball at all." ("How Do Athletes' Brains Control Their Movements?" *New York Times*, April 13, 2018, adapted from his *Performance Cortex: How Neuroscience Is Redefining Athletic Genius*; New York: E. P. Dutton, 2018).
9. See, for example, the 2015 documentary film *Fastball,* directed by Jonathan Hock and narrated by Kevin Costner.

epitomizes the power model of what pitchers are doing to hitters than the prevalence, throughout the baseball world, of the radar gun as a badge of a pitcher's quality.

Now, no doubt, the hard-thrown fastball is one of the pitcher's most valuable weapons. The intimidation factor alone is impressive. This is something you can experience in its rawest form in youth baseball. Kids play on smaller diamonds, and because they grow and get stronger at different rates, it is not uncommon for small children to find themselves facing already frightening fireball-throwing much bigger young men. This advantage is temporarily neutralized when the kids move up to bigger diamonds, for now the stronger pitcher has to work from farther back.

But what all this celebration of power and speed overlooks is that a fastball is only truly effective when it is used in combination with other pitches. It's easy (relatively speaking!) to hit a fastball if you know it's coming. You can tune yourself to it. But it is almost impossible to hit a fastball—or even for the backstop to catch it— if you don't know it's coming. And the same point goes in reverse. What makes a slow-pitched change-up so effective is the fact that you may be looking fastball and so are simply unable to hold back from swinging too soon.

Recall the lines from Robert Francis, quoted at this introduction's start: the pitcher's aim is "how not to hit the mark he seems to aim at," and "he throws to be a moment misunderstood." The pitcher is communicating with the batter, and his weapon is not so much speed and power—qualities easily measured by a number—as wile and indirection. Again, as Francis tells us, the pitcher's passion is "how to avoid the obvious." But his technique is "how to vary the avoidance." Batter and pitcher are in negotiation with each other, not with physics or neurophysiology; and their currency is not physical magnitudes like speed but all too human ones like deception and false expectations. To be successful, the batter needs to understand the pitcher, to appreciate his intentions. The pitcher for his part succeeds by "making the batter understand too late."

A numbers game? Not really. Quantities are external to what really matters in the at-bat.

The misguided celebration of the physical, the measurable, the mechanical, is to be found almost everywhere you look in baseball culture.

Take the case of the check-swing strike. Ron Darling, former Mets pitching star and now a member of their television broadcast team, mentioned on air recently that he asked an umpire to explain how umpires determine whether the batter has "come around" and so swung and missed on a check-swing strike. Is it the breaking of the wrists, or how far the arms move across the plate, he asked? Nah, the umpire said. It's none of that. What matters is whether the batter "offered at the pitch." That is, whether the batter *tried to hit the ball*. The umpire's concern, in other words, is not with a measurement of the batter's body but, rather, with a recognition of his intentions.

The very idea of the strike zone, so central to baseball reality, is widely misunderstood. These days MLB broadcasts boxlike visualizations of the strike zone ("pitchcast," or "statcast") overlaid on the tele-transmission so that we are shown, on screen, whether the ball is inside the drawn box or outside it. Commentators routinely call attention to the fact that a plate umpire's calls may fail to agree with the representation of the ball's location in the on-screen graphics. And of course there are those who would recommend replacing the umpire with a tennis-like, strike-calling device. But, as I discuss more later in the book, the umpire is *not* a measuring device; he's not an imperfect human ball-reading machine. He is a *judge*, or a referee, and what he cares about is not the exact physical location of the ball, but whether it is to the pitcher's credit that the batter couldn't hit the pitch, or whether it is the pitcher's fault that he threw a pitch the batter could not reasonably be expected even to try to hit. The strike zone is not so much a physical place as it is a zone of responsibility, and the job of the umpire is not to identify a ball's location in space but, rather, to adjudicate questions of should and could and ought. (Which is of course not to deny that a batter, or a spectator, may challenge the umpire's call on the grounds of the pitch's actual location. But the challenge, like the call itself, is a judgment about responsibility, credit, and blame.)

Or, to give yet a different kind of example, consider the recent truly misguided efforts on the part of baseball executives to, as they put it, "speed up the pace of play." The idea that baseball is too slow is based on the premise that only explosive plays and big hits count as action. But baseball is more subtle than home runs and double plays. When the batter steps out of the box and fixes his batting gloves, or weighs his bat, or scratches around in the box, he's not wasting time; he is surveying the situation before him, reading the signs, trying to figure out what pitch to look for. He is working. For the knowledgeable fan, these are moments of tactical complexity and high suspense. There's a lot going on and there's a lot for the spectator, together with the player, to try to appreciate. The same is true of mound visits by coaching staff. In those moments, the coach is like the corner guy in a boxing bout; with his words he makes it possible for the pitcher to keep on pitching.

It is a pity that the televised experience of the game tends to obscure the human drama by substituting in its place a merely pictorial one. But the pictorial view on things is also a detached view. The other day I witnessed a close play at home plate from up close. No camera angle or video replay was in the offing. I was present not to an image, but to movement and energy, an event or happening. The fact that the umpire was able confidently to make a call, to cope with the explosive reality before him, was an astonishing demonstration of his own skillfulness; he was actually participating in the action.

Baseball culture, when it comes to numbers, is in conflict with itself. In this, baseball is like the larger society of which it is a part. Baseball, as a historical matter, is a modern game; its origins are in the late nineteenth century. And its obsessions with numbers and measurement reflect the concerns of modern society with the same.

It is only in the late nineteenth century that natural science took something like its contemporary form. Before then, it was possible, at least as an aspirational ideal, for a single person to know everything. But by the late 1800s, this was no longer the case. If there was progress to be had in mathematics, chemistry, physics, physiology, astronomy, or geology, it was to be purchased by digging down deeper and deeper into pits of specialization. No doubt, the idea that the different sciences could all be unified— that they come down, in the end, to fundamental physics—has been fairly enshrined in scientific self-understanding for hundreds of years. But the fact is, by the end of the nineteenth century, science had become a community of different scientific subcultures, none of which could very easily be expected to communicate with the others. And each of which laid claim to its own distinct expertise.

The late nineteenth century also saw the arrival of brand-new would-be scientific disciplines such as sociology, economics, psychology, neurology, anthropology, and linguistics. What was distinctive about these new *human*, or social, sciences is that their claim to expertise extended beyond mere matters of theoretical knowledge to matters of direct importance to people and the society at large. And with their rise also came the expectation, or hope, or maybe fantasy, that society itself could be organized on scientific principles. This ideal was immortalized in the famous Manifesto of the Vienna Circle of 1929, in which the accomplishments of Einstein, Marx, and Freud were held up as models of a new scientific worldview.[10]

The fixation on the numbers in baseball is a reflection of this very same aspiration that it might be possible, finally, to identify value and harness action, on scientific principles.

I'm skeptical that hard science, positive knowledge, or numbers can serve in this way to ground the choices we face about what to do and how to live. What's the best way to raise your kids? Should you breastfeed? For how long? Should you let your kids cry themselves to sleep or should you soothe them? Is it okay for elementary school-age kids to spend hours playing with digital devices? There are lots of "experts" who will tell you what they think about

---

10. See *Wissenschaftliche Weltauffassung—Der Wiener Kreis,* by Rudolf Carnap, Hans Hahn, and Otto Neurath (Vienna: Wolf, 1929).

these and similar matters. But it would be unwise to think any one of them has the answer to *your* question—which is not, after all, what's best for kids but, rather, what *you* should do, what's best for *your* kid, here, now, in the situation in which you find yourself. What matters for you are your particulars and, of course, your values and commitments. And ditto for economics. We can't entrust the hard questions about a country's economic life to the experts. We, or our elected leaders, need to own the problems we face and make the hard choices ourselves.

Not that the experts don't have *piles* of information. It's just that the information doesn't add up to news we can use, or genuine knowledge. Or, rather, it's news we can use, but only at our own risk and with no guarantees. Caveat emptor.

And so with baseball. The thing about the pitcher who's just given up a hit and walked two batters to load the bases in a game-deciding situation is that his battle is with himself as much as it is with the opposing squad. And the manager's decision to leave him in, or call on a relief pitcher, is not one that can be decided by the numbers.

I almost cringe when I listen to the talking heads in Ken Burns's monumental baseball documentary wax sentimental and nostalgic about baseball, or when I read yet another scrivener explaining how baseball is the game of fathers and sons, how it is the greatest game there ever was, or the most beautiful, or the most fun, or the one that somehow most perfectly captures America's unique spirit. This is pretty discredited stuff, intellectually and politically. It's on a par, for example, with the unfortunately commonplace idea that some languages are somehow, by their very nature, better for love, or for humor, or for science.

Indeed, the whole idea that baseball is, or was, the *national pastime* strikes me as hard to believe. Are we supposed to imagine that a country so large as the United States, and made up of such a great diversity of population, can really be said to have been united in devotion to a single leisure activity? I suspect that the proposition that baseball is America's national pastime was never anything more than an unusually successful advertising slogan. Or we might better call it a piece of propaganda. And what makes advertising slogans and propaganda effective is not their truth but their power to change how we think—in this case, about ourselves. Just as advertising does not merely reflect but also influences our sense of what it is to be (for example) beautiful, and so comes even to mold how we feel about our own bodies, our own selves, so it seems to me the national pastime myth has shaped not only how we think about baseball but also how we feel about what it is to be American, including, for example, such things as what relationships between fathers and sons are supposed to look and feel like.

So whether or not baseball is or was the national pastime, this much is clear: baseball is tied, in fantasy at least, to an *idea* of America, to an idea of ourselves. Baseball is America's game, some of us feel compelled to say, and its history, its creation and evolution, are tied, for us, to a conception of ourselves (and to our own development as a nation and as a global superpower). This is why Jackie Robinson, a second baseman for the Brooklyn Dodgers, is revered as a national hero, and this is why our baseball championships, entirely domestic though they are, go by the name of the World Series.

Baseball is, in a sense, a myth, but we make it real by acting it out. We can see this, for example, when we turn back to the children at play. Organized youth baseball in the United States is an astonishing civic achievement. Fields are manicured, teams are constituted, games and tournaments scheduled, coaches and assistant coaches and team parents work hard for their teams. All this happens on a volunteer basis, in the spirit of community. So baseball isn't just an idea. It isn't just something we read about, or think about, or watch on TV. It's a real game, a game that is played by a lot of people. But crucially, notice that the renderings, depictions, transmissions, tellings and retellings of baseball that have historically filled our media airways and absorbed our attention tend, inexorably, to shape the way we play in their own image; all that— the writing and especially the TV—serves as the standard by which our live baseball play is actually experienced and evaluated.

Kids take up the batting stance of their professional idols; that is, they *pose* and what they imitate is an image they know from TV. When kids play ball, their every move and gesture is a kind of homage, and so, really, it is a mode of their participation in a picture culture, a media fantasy. The youth game's very organization— teams, uniforms, coaches, flags, anthems, and umps—is theater, or ritual, a participation in some idea of what it is we are supposed to be doing, as much as it is anything like spontaneous play. Baseball makes us in its image. And televised baseball is less a record of the way we play the game than it is the template of how we think we ought to be, how we ought to play.

Baseball, then, is as much pageant as play. It is a permanent audition. An exercise of collective aspiration. It is an image–reality loop. In this, it has more in common with Hollywood—another institution, in addition to modern science, that, like baseball, came of age in the early twentieth century—than it does with other sports. Like Hollywood, baseball is much more the *source* of the images in terms of which we understand ourselves, for better or for worse, than it is a record thereof.

None of which makes baseball false, or inauthentic.

This is what culture is. Culture is enactive, not real. By this I mean that the very concepts in terms of which we define our cultural identities—baseball, church, man, woman, gay, straight, Democrat, Republican—are never mere descriptors or categories; they are always also templates, or scripts, or scores, or models that we are disposed to live by.

Baseball does not imitate life itself, or our lives as members of a culture. Rather, baseball exemplifies our lives as members of a culture. We enact ourselves in baseball, as we enact ourselves in schools, or in the army, or in other regions of our social existence.

Far from making baseball inauthentic or false, the image–reality loop that is baseball actually makes baseball productive and un-bounded, infinite. Baseball really is a field of dreams. It is a figment in America's dream of itself, and America, in turn, understands it-self according to the shape of that dreamt-up thing we call baseball.

About the Trojan War, Homer wrote:

> The gods
> devised and measured out this devastation,
> to make a song for those in times to come.[11]

This brings us closer to the truth about baseball. We play baseball so that we may sing and write about it.

---

11. Homer, *The Odyssey*, translated by Emily Wilson (New York: Norton, 2018).

In Praise of Being Bored

1 | DO WE NEED TO SPEED UP BASEBALL?

Major League Baseball (MLB) is wrestling with the question of how to shorten the length of baseball games.

It is eager to find ways to speed things up. The *New York Times* not long ago invited staff writers and readers to offer suggestions, and was inundated with ideas ranging from the reasonable (such as stricter enforcement of timeouts) to the unrealistic (lopping off innings of play, making it two strikes and you're out, or letting teams change the batting order late in the game).

The history of baseball is a history of rule changes. The mound was lowered after 1968 as a response to too dominant pitching; the foul/strike rule—making some foul balls count as strikes—was introduced earlier in the twentieth century to counter the opposite problem: the failure of pitchers to contain hitting. These were changes introduced to improve the game and level the playing field in the face of shifting styles of play and shifting technologies (new balls, for example). They represent a real evolution of the game. They also, inevitably, introduce an element of incommensurability when it comes to comparing on-field accomplishments across different eras. The extraordinary pitching accomplishments of Bob Gibson, Sandy Koufax, and others were made possible, at least in part, by conditions of play that no longer remain. Or consider the fact that prior to 1920, the most homers hit in a season was 29— by Babe Ruth. After 1920, offensive statistics boomed, in large part because of changes in the way balls were handled during play (inaugurating the so-called live-ball era).

The rule changes now contemplated are of an entirely different kind. They aren't designed to improve the game but, rather, to improve the product. I can't second-guess Major League Baseball's analysis of marketing realities and its economic interests. I'll defer to their expertise when it comes to knowing how to maximize revenue. If the people want a faster game, well, then, give 'em what they want.

But I think they are making a big mistake nonetheless. What makes baseball boring—and I agree that lots of people think baseball is boring—is the same thing that makes classical music or physics boring (to some people): it's difficult. It takes knowledge and focus to understand what's happening on the baseball field. Every juncture is the intersection of multiple decisions. What to pitch? How to position the fielders? Where to make the play? And the answers to these questions depend on the situation specifics— and are sensitive to endless complication. Are there men on base? Who's batting, and who's on base? Who's on the mound? How fresh is he? What's the situation on the bench? Who's on deck? And on and on.

It takes not only experience but also curiosity and patience to realize what's at play in a baseball game. For one who can perceive all this, the game is anything but slow. In fact, it's way too fast. You've got to be quick to keep track of what's going on so that you don't get stuck making decisions too late.

It takes time to follow and understand the game, and it takes time to play the game—and to play the game well. Batters and base runners and fielders have a lot to think about, a lot to understand. The game has evolved techniques of distributed decision-making. Managers signal catchers who guide pitchers; they relay messages to coaches who communicate with hitters and runners and fielders. It looks like they're all just standing around scratching themselves. In fact, they are hard at work, deliberating, communicating, deciding. And delivering action in real time.

Of course, it's a slow sport. It's gotta be slow. But that's not slow *boring*. Not for the players. And not for the fans who both understand and empathize with the players.

Consider the showdown between pitcher and batter known as the "at-bat." For each of them, this is it; it's his chance, an epic opportunity for self-actualization. The pitcher has to risk everything and dare the batter to swing at pitches he can't hit, with the eyes of the world, and those of every player or person in the ballpark, upon him. The batter, for his part, faces the puzzle of figuring out what the pitcher is going to do; unless he knows in advance, he doesn't have much chance of hitting anything. The ball moves too fast. His problem is physical, but it's also intellectual and highly stressful. He, too, is in the spotlight. Why shouldn't he step out of the batter's box to refasten his batting gloves? He's doing everything he can to focus, to find a way to be present and in control in a difficult situation.

A comparison with Little Leaguers will help. A Little Leaguer at bat doesn't call timeout between every pitch. He has to be *taught* to use stepping out of the box as a way of settling himself down and taking control of the battle, the bout, the dance he is caught up in with the pitcher. The pitcher, too, needs to find a way to let go of what has, maybe, just gone wrong and maintain focus on his current task: using his body to hurl a ball to a narrow little target. The pitcher needs to learn to breathe, to organize, to keep control of the pace of play.

Now, if you don't know what you're seeing, if you don't understand the tactical minutiae constraining every little thing these guys are doing—and if you don't appreciate the difficulty and stress they are under—well, then, yeah, it doesn't look like much is going on. Or maybe you just aren't even really paying attention, multitasking as you may be with your smartphone. Boredom is the fruit of your disconnect, your disengagement.

But speeding up the play is not a remedy for this kind of boredom that is born of disengagement and indifference.

The managers and curators at our art museums face exactly these challenges. The art may be as good as it gets. The curious thing, though, is that it can't speak for itself. It's as if every work, no matter how great, no matter what, is in the "standby" mode until you, the viewer, figure out how to turn it on—that is, figure out what to look at, think about, and pay attention to. So how can the museum assist you in figuring out how to turn the work on? How can it make the work accessible to you? Wall text may help, but it can also distract. Audio guides can be an instrument for helping you figure out what to care about. But they can just as easily get in the way of your actually seeing anything at all. A lot of museums produce shows these days as if the show is really just the backdrop for the real experience, which is the chance to buy branded products. Gift shops are situated in museums like duty-free shops in airports. They are a place for people to relax, stop working, and do what comes more easily: spend money. They are a relief from the art.

Baseball is a business, so I don't doubt for a minute that revenue will guide decisions about the future of the game. But I would invite the decision-makers to pause long enough to realize what is at stake. Baseball is a game of ideas.

The problem baseball faces isn't that it goes too slow. The problem is that it doesn't go slow enough. Players and spectators alike need to slow down and let baseball happen.

2 | IN PRAISE OF BEING BORED

When Bud Selig, who was then commissioner of baseball—he served from 1998 through 2015—visited Oakland in the summer of 2014, he took the opportunity to bemoan the A's inadequate stadium and also to worry aloud about a topic that seems to loom large in the minds of many baseball administrators these days—namely, the increasingly slow pace of the game.

Indeed, the game has gotten slower over time.

A game today lasts, on average, more than 30 minutes longer than it did thirty years ago. I suspect the big culprit here is longer commercial breaks (between 30 and 40 minutes of a baseball game broadcast). And then there is also the recent institution of instant replay. But the target of Selig's concern, it seems, was the players themselves. They're just playing too slowly, he complained. Too much time elapses between pitches. Too many timeouts to adjust equipment or wardrobe.

Selig, in my opinion, is wrong on both counts. The A's have a great stadium. And baseball does not move too slowly.

As for the pace of the game, I am a bit surprised that MLB is concerned about this at all. Revenues are up, TV viewing is up, there are more teams than ever, and most of them are very rich. If you measure the sport's vitality in business terms, baseball, it would seem, has never been better. And if you visit the ballpark to watch a game, it's immediately clear that today's live baseball experience positively thrives on interruptions to the play. That's when you get to spend your money.

What exactly is the problem?

Don't say: "The game is too slow; it's getting boring."

As anyone who knows and loves baseball will tell you, baseball *is* boring. This is nothing new. Even at its most lively best, baseball is a game that unfolds at a walking pace, or at the pace of a relaxed conversation. When compared to the unstopping swarm dynamic of soccer or hockey, or the drive and dance of basketball, baseball hardly even seems like a sport at all.

And this is what the great many of us who love baseball love about it. Baseball games aren't just long. There's no way of knowing how long they might be. A baseball game, like a good conversation, or a friendship, or a political controversy, has no fixed end. It takes however long it takes. As Selig observed, baseball is a game without a clock. And that's a good thing.

Selig also questions whether this kind of unstructured, open time is palatable in today's fast-paced world.

I say, God save us from today's ramped-up, multi-interrupted, selfie-consumed, fast-paced world! We need to slow down. We need to turn off. We need to unplug. We need to start things and not know when they are going to end. We need evenings at the ballpark, evenings spent outside of real time.

What's so bad about being bored?

I found myself at a table with Europeans the other night. The topic turned to the relative merits of baseball and what they call "football." I had to restrain myself from expressing my irritation.

It isn't that there isn't a boatload to be said about how these sports differ from each other. And it is certainly true that we love our own sports and may find ourselves actively disliking the sports of others. For example, I admit that I found myself losing interest in World Cup Soccer once the players advanced from flopping around on the floor in throes of pretend agony (in an effort to induce a foul call) to actually biting each other.[1]

But the thing is, arguing about sports is like arguing about foods. We like what we grew up with; kids around the world aren't soccer fans because, after having surveyed the world's sports, they chose soccer. And the same goes for Americans and baseball. We don't like our sports because they're great. They are great because we like them. Or, maybe, loving a sport—coming to understand it—lets you see the greatness that otherwise goes unwitnessed.

As for Selig's judgment on the A's stadium, I agree it's an old concrete-and-steel throwback to another era. True, there are no roller coasters, or hot tubs, or extensive gourmet food offerings. And yes, you can see the faded paint of the Raiders' gridiron running across the A's diamond.

But the A's home field is a fabulous place to watch baseball. It may not be a top-of-the-line shopping mall and entertainment center, but it is a spacious, open cathedral of baseball. It is a place where baseball happens and where you just may find, if you are lucky, that you have the opportunity to relax and get bored.

---

1. Recall the case of Uruguay's Luis Suarez, who bit an Italian defender during World Cup play in 2014.

3 | THREE CHEERS FOR INSTANT REPLAY

The San Francisco Giants challenged a call in Game 7 of the 2014 World Series against the Kansas City Royals. With no outs and a runner on first, Eric Hosmer, the Royals first baseman, smacked a grounder up the middle. Joe Panik, second baseman for the Giants, dived to his right, found the ball, and tossed it from his gloved hand to the shortstop, who fired the ball to first in an attempt to seal the double play. Hosmer, who had dived head-first, was called safe. Bruce Bochy, the Giants manager, challenged the call. It took the umpiring crew—in conference with the umpires holed up in the video monitoring station in New York City's Chelsea neighborhood—almost three minutes to overturn the on-field decision. Eventually they called the runner out at first, giving the Giants a potentially game-changing double play.

The play-by-play announcers bemoaned the fact that the review took so long. Baseball's slow pace had itself been under review by a committee of experts assembled by baseball's outgoing commissioner, Bud Selig. But the announcers seem to have missed the real story: those three minutes were *thrilling*. It was high drama. It wasn't an interruption in the play; it extended the play to a whole new level.

The interruption gave us all a chance to try to reach a decision about what had happened—safe or out? And it also provided an opportunity to get clear about the elements of the play. Why did the runner dive head-first into first, anyway? Wouldn't it have been faster if he'd kept on sprinting? And also *noisier*; the sound of the foot hitting the bag, like that of the ball smacking the first baseman's mitt, is a crucial source of information for the umpire about who reached the bag first—ball or runner?

The play review also gave us the chance to reconsider just what the middle infielders had managed to accomplish in making the play so close. Panik's snag was a play for the ages. And Giant shortstop Brandon Crawford turnaround was outstanding. The play had been challenged because it was close and because it was important. Replay gave us time to understand what was going on.

My worry about instant replay had never been that it wouldn't work—that it wouldn't succeed in correcting errors on the part of umpiring. My worry was always that it would work too well. Baseball is not now, and has never been, about mere facts. Ball or strike, fair or foul. Baseball is not tennis. Baseball is about what *people* do, about what they accomplish in the social setting of the game, and so, it has always been concerned with the conversation itself, the debate, the process of adjudication. Umpires are part of the game, just as lawyers and police are part of the society they patrol. The umpires are players, too.

Now that we've had time to see baseball's instant-review challenge system at work, it's clear that my worries were misplaced; the new rules enhance the umpires' role instead of limiting it, as I had feared. Remember: pictures, even slow-motion films, don't decide anything for you. They just give you more information on the basis of which to reach a decision. I am amazed how difficult it is to tell, even in slow-mo, whether runners are safe or out. It's always a judgment call—and instant replay doesn't change that.

It's still the umpires, the same guys who work the field, making the hard calls. Using slow-motion replay to evaluate and re-evaluate plays actually amplifies the challenges. And that's a good thing. Every challenge is an invitation to think about the game and understand it better.

I was a naysayer when instant replay was introduced. But now I'm a proponent. Not because it makes the game fairer. But because it makes it more fun.

4 | THE PROBLEM WITH BASEBALL ON TV

I watch a fair bit of baseball on TV. But watching on TV pales beside the experience of watching a game in the ballpark.

Why should this be? The camera lets you see things you can't see even from the best seat in the house. Shouldn't the televised experience be better?

Here's a clue. I am always struck, when I bring my kids to the stadium, that they can't see the game. It's not that there's anything wrong with their eyesight. They are remarkably sensitive to the approach of hot dog and soda vendors. And when it comes to detecting the onset of a cotton-candy buying opportunity, their powers of discernment far surpass my own. But the action on the field? It's out of reach.

The developmental psychologist Linda B. Smith has studied what toddlers look at when they play with toys on a table top. One of her findings is that little kids see and pay attention to what they are holding. This isn't surprising. As she noted in a recent talk I heard her give, kids' arms are short. To hold something is, in effect, to hold it directly before the eyes. The first perceptual horizon is pegged to the arms' length.

As we get older, we acquire suites of skills and knowledge and interests that, like the child's arms, allow us to grab onto things and bring them into focus. It won't be long before my kids will read the news every day to find out what's happening on the other side of the globe. Think of how much they need to learn, how much they need to know how to do, before that activity could have any point for them!

One of the big mistakes we make is to think that seeing is optical. It isn't. Seeing is a matter of understanding and caring.

And it is also an achievement. To watch a game in person and follow what's going on is, when you think about it, a dazzling cognitive accomplishment. I love baseball, but I never cease to be humbled by all the stuff I miss when I don't have the guidance of the professional announcer's play-by-play to keep me fixed on what matters.

And that's the point. When you watch a game on TV, someone else—the producers and commentators—does the work for you. They tell you what to pay attention to and what not to pay attention to. They digest the reality on the field for you. They deliver a story with a tidy script.

But the real joy of watching baseball—the joy of watching or learning about anything!—is discerning what's happening yourself. Watching sports on TV is passive and sedative, rather than inventive and energetic.

Or, at least, it can be. The fact that TV organizes the game for you can open up new opportunities; for example, it can free you to pay attention to subtleties of strategy that might seem remote when you're in the crowd. But it's important to remember that

TV—which has a seeming unlimited power to hold us captive—imposes real costs as well.

It is too easy, when watching something on TV—baseball, or anything else—to think you are seeing it when you are not.

5 | JOINT ATTENTION

Imagine this: it's Game 7 of the 2015 World Series. Matt Harvey is on the mound for the New York Mets. He reaches a two-strike count against one of the Royals' batters. And then something expected but at the same time utterly amazing happens: the whole stadium—as if with a single mind—rises to its feet and roars with excitement and encouragement. Forty thousand people act in unison, as if governed by one and the same external force, or as if subject to the whim of an omnipotent choreographer.

Of course, there is no mystery here. It is the shared interest of the fans in the action unfolding on the field, and their understanding of it, that unites them and brings them into such striking coordination. No doubt the impulse to jump up and scream is also caused, in part, by the fact that so many people around you are doing it, too.

What unifies the fans, what organizes them and brings them into coordination, is their shared understanding and shared attention.

Compare this with a different kind of case of human coordination: a work of large-scale dance choreography. As an example, consider Heiner Goebbels's *Surrogate Cities,* which I saw performed by the Berliner Philharmoniker under the direction of Sir Simon

Rattle, with choreography by Matthilde Monnier, in Berlin in 2008. In this work of contemporary music and dance, hundreds of nonprofessional dancers, spread out over a great hall, move in exact unison. The perfect harmony of movement, combined with the obvious fact that these were not professional dancers but ordinary folk, was astonishing to see—and also puzzling. How did the choreographer pull it off? How did she train them so well?

The secret, it turned out, was that there were monitors positioned, teleprompter-like, around the space in such a way that the dancers could see them—but the audience could not. Each dancer had a fairly simple task: to imitate the action performed on screen, with no concern at all for timing or coordination with others.

While they were unified by a common task—to do what the person on the monitor was doing—there was no significant cross-coordination among them. Each person would have done whatever the person on the screen was doing, whatever anybody else was doing. Their harmony reflected the common cause of their movements, rather than any intention to coordinate, or even the slightest ability to do so.

Here, in contrast with the baseball spectacle, there is no shared understanding or shared attention. True, all the dancers *are* paying attention to a monitor. But for all that it mattered, each dancer might have had his or her own private monitor. They were, in effect, acting alone together. Which is an interesting idea. *Surrogate Cities* was commissioned to celebrate the 1,200-year anniversary of the city of Frankfurt and is a work about urban life. "Alone together" captures part of that, no doubt.

Consider another well-studied phenomenon: when people talk, they tend to take up similar positions, postures, and tilts;

they settle on a shared loudness, and they are likely to adopt a common dialect. Talking is like dancing. It is spontaneous and, yet, it is also habitual. It is organized in all sorts of subtle, not-quite-conscious-nor-yet-fully-unconscious ways.

This is one reason why talking to one of your passengers while you are driving is not particularly distracting, although talking to someone over the telephone while you are driving *is*. You and your passenger organize yourself in relation to your shared, common situation; your passenger's movements, crucially, like your own, are sensitive to what is happening around you (both). Talking on the phone—whether using a handheld device or not—forces you to split your attention. It's interesting that radio does not distract in this way. This is because, owing to the passivity of our attitude toward radio, it doesn't entrain us in a conversation-like way. It keeps safely in the background.

It is astonishing to realize how—and in how many different ways—we are coordinated.

The next time you are at the ballpark, take a moment to appreciate how profoundly you share your experience with those around you.

Keeping Score

6 | THE FORENSIC SPORT

People like to say that baseball is a game of statistics, but really it is a game of law. It is a *forensic* sport.

When I say baseball is a forensic sport, what I mean is this: in baseball we are interested less in what happens than in who is liable, or responsible, for what happens; we are interested in apportioning praise and blame. To put it better, in baseball—as in the law—the way you determine *what happened* is by making a judgment about who is responsible for what happened.

Whether an act of violent killing is murder depends on the halo of circumstances surrounding the act. We can know the local facts—A shot and killed B, say—and still not know for sure whether A *murdered* B. Was it an accident? Was it self-defense? Was it an act of passion, or a mercy killing, or an act of war? *What was done* depends, we can say, on *more* than just what was done.

And so with baseball. Batter hits ball and makes it safely to first base. What we want to know is, *Did he get a hit?* And this is really the question: Did he *earn* the base, or did he get it as a result of a fielder's choice or a fielder's error? Do we praise him for his achievement and so credit *him* with the achievement? Or do we blame the fielder for what happened and so deprive the batter of having gotten a hit at all? What happens, in baseball, is constituted by matters forensic, matters of praise and blame.

Consider: runs are either *earned* or *unearned*. That ball that got away from the catcher and allowed a runner to advance a base? It is either a wild pitch, and is the pitcher's fault, or it is a *passed ball*, which is the catcher's mistake. Did that runner *steal* the base, or did he take it thanks to *defensive indifference*? Some pitches are *strikes* and others are *balls*. That is, some pitches are pitches the batter *ought to be able to hit*—he's to blame if he fails to do so—and some are just lousy throws for which the pitcher is liable.

Generally we blame a batter if he doesn't get a hit. But not always. In cases where the pitcher fails to give him a good pitch and he is awarded a free base, or where he flies out to score a runner (a sacrifice), we treat the batter as if he did not even have an "at-bat." He is rewarded with a free pass, of sorts.

Nothing brings out the forensic character of baseball—and its broad significance—so much as the practice, in baseball, of *keeping score*.

In baseball—and here the contrast with most other sports is great—keeping score is never just a matter of keeping track of who's winning. It's a matter of notating, in the thick evaluative sense I've been trying to bring out, *exactly what happened*, play by play, during a game. This isn't easy to do; it requires patience, concentration, and more than anything else, knowledge and understanding of the game. It requires the skills of a *judge*.

Now we come to the heart of the matter. The baseball scorekeeper's text is never merely a record of the game. There is no such thing as a *complete* record of what happened, after all. And anyway, who needs a complete record? It's not as though it would make sense to *play* a baseball score the way musicians might play a musical score. Not even in the imagination.

No, in a way the practice of scorekeeping in baseball—the practice of trying to write baseball down, which is to say, trying to make sense of it—is the point of the game itself.

Baseball, when all is said and done, is, or at least incorporates, a writing practice.

Baseball serves to remind us that the project of trying to write ourselves is important and ongoing.

7 | NO-HITTERS, PERFECT GAMES, AND THE MEANING OF LIFE

On June 1, 2012, Johan Santana threw a no-hitter for the New York Mets. It was his first. More remarkably, it was the first Mets no-hitter ever. Santana succeeded where Tom Seaver, Nolan Ryan, and Doc Gooden had failed. For baseball lovers, a no-hitter is a thing of beauty. For Mets fans (like me), Santana's achievement was a cause for jubilation

A little less than two weeks later, Matt Cain, the San Francisco Giants pitcher who'd recently signed a huge multi-year contract, performed an even rarer feat. He pitched a perfect game. A perfect game is one in which, from the point of view of the pitcher who is credited with throwing it, nothing bad happens. It's 27 men up, 27 men down.

As a general rule, sports are about winning and losing. We judge performance by the bottom line. Points, goals, touchdowns, etc. But not baseball.

Sure, the winner is the team with the most runs, however they come about. But in baseball we also take up a different perspective and ask not "What happened?" but, rather, "Who is responsible for what happened?" Did the batter get on base through his own achievement, or as a result of someone else's mistake? That is, did he get a hit? Did the runner steal second base, or did he merely take it owing to the indifference of the defenders, in which case his action, though materially the same, does not count as a steal? We individuate events in baseball in relation to the question of credit and blame. What is a strike, really, but a pitch that a batter ought to be able to hit and that therefore counts against him if he fails to hit it?

The point is, baseball is preoccupied with agency. It is a forensic sport, as I have been arguing. It is, at bottom, a kind of experiment in responsibility. That's what makes it so fascinating.

Take the case of the no-hitter. What makes a no-hitter special is not that the opposing team fails to get on base or score runs; what makes it special is that you can't blame the pitcher for the bad stuff that happens to his team; he *gives up* no hits and so he can't be faulted for what the other team may or may not achieve. Suppose the batter gets to first on a dropped third strike, advances to second on a ground-out, and then to third on a passed ball, eventually scoring on a sacrifice fly ball caught deep in the outfield. It is not the pitcher's fault that the run scored. Yes, the opponents score the run, but, crucially, they don't earn it.

Wait a second, you might object, we certainly can and will blame the pitcher if—as with Santana's no-hitter—he walks numerous batters, or if he hits a batter with a pitch and so gives him a base. Yes. But what's telling here is that, at least in traditional baseball thinking, the batter himself gets no credit for walking or getting hit by a pitch; these don't even count as "at-bats." If the batter deserves no credit for accomplishing something, then surely the pitcher can't be blamed for what the batter actually does. And that's what we are signaling when we applaud the pitcher's no-hitter: not merely success but also a certain blamelessness and so a certain praiseworthiness.

A no-hitter is special because in baseball, as in life, we sometimes care less about what happens—who's actually winning or losing—than about who is accountable. Nothing brings this out more than the fact that it is possible to lose a no-hitter; indeed, this has happened. Its quality, its value as an achievement, floats free of outcomes.

Sometimes life is like a no-hitter. Outcomes are sometimes less important than intentions, purposes, reasons. For example, it is not the deed, but, really, the intention that marks the differences between murder, justifiable homicide, and accidental killing.

Things are just the other way around with a perfect game. A no-hitter is perfect when it is not only the case that the pitcher lets no bad stuff happen (e.g., gives up no hits) but also no one else does, either. A perfect game is special because sometimes we care primarily about outcomes; we applaud the pitcher not only because he gave up no hits but also because he got lucky; the stars lined up and the enemy was vanquished.

A perfect game is so easily spoiled. An errant throw, a booted ground ball, an umpire's bad call. A game is only perfect when everyone on the field is perfect.

Sometimes life is like a perfect game. Outcomes can be all that matters. Murder, justifiable homicide, accidental killing. These are different names for the act of killing a human being, aren't they?

I think baseball fans tend to think that no-hitters are great but perfect games are correspondingly greater, rarer, more special. A perfect game, from this point of view, is thought of just as a very special kind of no-hitter. It is a no-hitter *plus*.

But actually no-hitters and perfect games are entirely different kinds of achievements, with incommensurable values. We credit a pitcher for a perfect game the way we credit the president for the nation's prosperity. It's not that he's really responsible. He got lucky, and he got out of the way and let luck do its work. And so with the pitcher.

The pitcher of a perfect game is admirable because he is blessed. Not so the pitcher of a no-hitter. His achievement is all his own; it is earned. But in the end it is really nothing more than *his* achievement; it doesn't even guarantee his victory or that of his team.

My point is not that the pitcher of a no-hitter could have done it alone. Of course not. It is a general truth about human accomplishment that we manage what we manage only against the background of the situation in which we find ourselves, a situation that inevitably includes others. A self-made businessperson must rely on so many other people, and so many institutions and structures for which he or she can take no direct responsibility (roads, utilities, etc.), just to get to the point of deserving to be called "self-made." And so with no-hitters. Behind every no-hitter there is a sound defense. Indeed, there have been no-hitters in which the pitcher had no strikeouts (e.g., the case of the Chicago Cubs' Kenny Holtzman in 1969); in such a game, every single out was made on a ball in play! And of course many a no-hitter has been saved by a great or unlikely play in the field, or perhaps, even, as in fact happened in the case of Santana, by a piece of questionable officiating.

But the fact remains: we credit a pitcher for getting a side out, even when batters manage to put balls in play. And this is not only because we feel we are entitled to take a competent, if not a perfect, defense for granted but also because we credit the pitcher for, if you like, keeping the batted balls in play.

Crucially, it is not the pitcher's skill, focus, or domination alone that makes the difference between a no-hitter and a perfect game. A perfect game truly is an accomplishment of the whole team.

Baseball, like the law, is an arena in which we investigate these competing ways of thinking about life, what we do, and what matters.

8 | KEEPING SCORE

Who keeps a scorecard by hand at baseball games these days? Fewer and fewer people, according to press reports. Why bother when you can enjoy a live play-by-play on your handheld device? And if you insist on keeping score yourself, there are apps you can download that make it much easier than doing it by hand.

Maybe the biggest reason so few people keep score these days—or even stay put in their seats watching the game for more than a few innings at a time—is that a day at the ballpark isn't just about baseball anymore (if it ever was). Games and videos on the scoreboard, deafening music, high-priced food and drink, shops and playgrounds. And then, of course, so many of us have multipurpose entertainment systems in our pockets. All these compete with the baseball for your attention.

But you do still see a few old codgers—and the occasional young one, like my son—sitting there with a scoresheet spread out on their laps, carefully writing down the plays. The real fanatics may be listening to the game on the radio (although these days, more likely than not, live-streamed over the internet).

Why do they insist on doing this? What are they doing? Why keep score?

The answer, I believe, goes way beyond baseball. Scorekeeping is a conceptually rich and important practice.

One person interviewed for a recent article in the *New York Times* said he had no interest in the "hard work" of keeping score. "Too much to write down. I have live ESPN gamecast. It keeps me updated."[1]

This brings us to the heart of the matter. This guy got it all wrong. Granted, scorekeeping is hard work. But we don't keep score to keep track or to keep updated.

Consider, first, that keeping score is not just a matter of recording the game. It is, rather, a way of thinking about the game. The scorekeeper asks, What is happening? Is that an earned run? Did the runner reach first on a fielder's choice, or did he get a hit? Is that a sacrifice, or was the batter bunting for a hit? In order to keep score, you need to make these kinds of evaluations and decisions. And in order to make these kinds of calls you need to be closely engaged with the game. You need to pay attention. You need to understand what is going on. You need to have skill. You need to care.

Notice: you can't write *everything* down. Do you score every pitch? Even the foul balls? Do you note down where the fielders are positioned at each moment in the game? Do you keep track of the amount of time between pitches?

You can't write everything down. But nor do you need to. Writing the game—keeping score—isn't about *reproducing* the

---

1. Harvey Araton, "Who Scores Games by Hand Anymore?," *New York Times*, July 11, 2013.

game, or even recording it. It's about understanding the game. Thinking about it. Keeping score.

(What you do decide to keep track of will depend on your interests. The pitching coach—or the pitcher's mom—*will* carefully score each pitch.)

But there is a second point that deserves our attention. The scorekeeper doesn't stand apart from the game, merely describing it. The game consists of what the players are doing. But it is the scorekeeper who decides, literally, what the players are doing. For example, the scorekeeper asks: Should the third baseman have fielded that grounder? If the answer is yes, then it follows that he, in fact, just committed an error. For the rest of us, this can have the consequence that the pitcher's no-hitter is intact. The activity of keeping score is in this way internal to the game itself.

Now, in practice, we treat one person's scorecard—that of the official scorekeeper—as canonical. So, in a sense, when the rest of us keep score, we are just taking notes. The official scorekeeper, in contrast, is doing something very different: he or she is shaping events in real time as they occur. The official scorer isn't just keeping score; he or she is, if you'll permit the wordplay, composing one.

Yes. But at the same time let us note that the official scorekeeper's authority is purely conventional. He or she has no special powers and no privileged access to the events on the field. And surely we can allow that it is possible for him or her to be mistaken.

This means that we can't let ourselves off the hook. There is no official telling of the French Revolution or the Iraq War; how could there be? Each of us has the right, but also in some sense the obligation, to make sense of events as we know them.

And so, I think, with baseball. Neither the folks at ESPN, nor the official scorer, nor the announcers on TV, have the authority to decide history for you and me. In baseball as in life, each of us has to keep his or her own scorecard. If we want to know what's going on, that is.

Which brings us to a final, crucial point.

Keeping score, in baseball or in life, is a knowledge-making activity. It is, we might say, a form of research. We can get by just fine reading along on the ESPN gamecast or taking the evening newscast at face value. For most of us, most of the time, that's the best we can manage. But there is another option: we can keep score—that is, we can write the events that matter to us. We can make knowledge; we can make history.

How we keep score—using an app, writing it out by hand, or even just in conversation—is irrelevant. But *that* we keep score, or that at the very least we recognize that the score needs keeping—that we can't, however much we might like, abdicate our authority to make sense of what is going on—is crucial.

It would indeed be a dark consequence of life in the digital age if we forgot that keeping score is more than keeping track, and that each of us has the power to keep score.

9 | THE NUMBERS GAME

Since the Enlightenment, champions of progress have urged us to break free of the chains of tradition.

Just because "we've always done it this way" is no reason to keep doing it this way. According to the champions of progress, it is irrational, it is stupid, indeed, it is frequently dishonest, to cling to traditions. If we aim to understand the world and control it—and this, surely, is the abiding ambition of all rational, empirically minded people—then we must rid ourselves of the baggage of inherited convention.

Keith Law's book *Smart Baseball* brings this revolutionary spirit of the Enlightenment to the topic of baseball. Law's topic is the importance of new methods of statistical analysis for clear thinking about the game.[1] But it's hard not to be struck by the fervor with which Law makes the case that in baseball an irrational tradition shackles progressive thinking. And it strikes me that more than just baseball is at stake. What is at stake, finally, is the

---

1. Keith Law, *Smart Baseball: The Story Behind the Old Stats That Are Ruining the Game, the New Ones That Are Running It, and the* Right *Way to Think About Baseball* (New York: HarperCollins, 2017).

Enlightenment aspiration of putting math and science, the numbers, to work in evaluating and predicting human achievement.

For Law, the "old stats" threaten to ruin the game. Batting average, for example, is a terrible measure of a batter's offensive "value," since it considers hits per at-bat. This is doubly wrongheaded, he contends: it ignores the fact that not all hits are created equal (a home run is worth more than a single), and it disregards the batter's offensive achievements (e.g., walks), which don't happen during at-bats (since not all plate appearances count as at-bats). Likewise, Runs Batted In is not only an uninformative measure of how good a player is offensively, but it is also dishonest, for it confuses his accomplishment with those of his teammates, Law says. You can only drive batters in, after all, if there are runners on base to be driven in.

Or consider the evaluation of pitching performance by wins; this is even more outrageous, he says. You can only win if your team scores, and the pitcher has no control over that. The idea that it is the pitcher who wins is premised, Law seems to think, on the idea that good pitchers have a kind of magic that leads their teams to victory. And that, Law is certain, is so much nonsense.[2] Praising an individual player for results over which he has nothing resembling control isn't very bright. It isn't going to help you figure out

---

2. Jacob deGrom, the Mets pitcher, finished the 2018 season with a 10-9 win-loss record. And yet it is universally acknowledged that his was one of the top two or three best, if not the best, performances in baseball that year. The weak record is no reflection of his pitching excellence—a 1.70 ERA and 269 strikeouts over 217 innings pitched—but of the staggeringly poor quality of his team's offense. In fact, he went on to be awarded the 2019 National League Cy Young Award.

what's really going on the field, and might very well lead you to make bad baseball decisions.

We use statistics, Law holds, to evaluate performance. We want to understand what a player *actually does* on the field, and we want to predict likely performance going forward. We need objectivity to do this. We need data. We need metrics that cut through the noise to the reality. The last thing we need are old-fashioned prejudices about pitchers winning games and RBIs being a measure of a player's offensive value to his team.

Can we do what Law and his fellow "quants" demand? Can we use numbers to assign value, to sort through praise and blame, and to ground baseball decisions in matters of value-neutral fact? I get it that this is something baseball executives want. Michael Lewis explained in his book *Moneyball* that the new statistics make it possible to discover sources of baseball value that traditional thinking has tended to ignore.[3] And as Alan Schwarz reminds us in *The Numbers Game,* this is nothing new.[4] Baseball has been grappling with how to use the numbers to ground baseball decision-making since the very beginning. And I certainly get it that if you're a player, or a manager, or a fan, the problem of evaluating and predicting is of the greatest importance.

But is it actually possible, in baseball or in life, so to regiment, to comprehend, and to control human behavior?

I am skeptical.

---

3. Michael Lewis, *Moneyball* (New York: Norton, 2003).
4. Alan Schwarz, *The Numbers Game: Baseball's Lifelong Fascination with Statistics* (New York: St. Martin's, 2004).

One of the things that particularly bugs Law about the RBI stat is that there are cases, as he notes, where the official scorer has discretion over whether to award the RBI. He explains:

> any stat that involves such human objectivity [I think he meant to write "subjectivity"] is immediately reduced in value as a result. People are prone to so many cognitive biases and are so inconsistent in their judgments that allowing them to award or withhold an RBI seems like far too much responsibility. (33)

But in fact, I would argue, all baseball statistics rest, at the end of the day, on exactly this sort of subjectivity. Consider that at the lowest level, baseball is about hits and outs. Law makes this point himself; as he explains, the basic job of a batter is to *not make an out*—that is, to get on base.

What makes something an out? Are outs determined in an objective way? Not really. Typically, the question of whether an out was made is a judgment call. Instant replay, it's worth noting, hasn't changed this. It only removes the required judgment to a remote location.

And the same is true of hits themselves. When is a hit a hit, and when is it, for example, the result of a fielder's error? Nothing determines this other than the decision of the official scorer (decisions which seem to be governed by convention, to a large extent; for instance, what is the rationale for refusing to call it an error when a outfielder loses the ball in the lights, but not when he lets the ball pop out of his glove?).

And let's not even get into balls and strikes!

However you look at it, the low-level facts on the ground, the smallest units of meaningful baseball—hits, outs, balls, strikes, foul or fair—are themselves soft, squishy, value-laden matters of interpretation.

Bring the biggest quantificational cannon you can find. It won't shoot straight if you set it down on shifting sands.

I suspect that this is not a bad thing. Baseball's concern is never primarily descriptive but, rather, always interpretive, and quantitative analysis can't change this, or give us a reason to want to change this. In baseball, we are called on to evaluate, to make choices, to make predictions, to lay odds precisely when there are, and indeed because there are, no algorithms or mathematical rules to do this for us.

I am no reactionary and I don't advocate a return to tradition. I think Law and his fellow "quants" are right that there is value in new analytical tools for thinking about baseball. But that's a far cry from accepting the idea that it is possible to use numbers, by themselves, to identify and control value, in baseball or anywhere else.

Want to know what happened on the field? You'd better take a look, and give it some thought.

The Communication Game

10 | BASEBALL AND THE NATURE OF LANGUAGE

Mine is an unusual name. I have come to learn that it is isn't possible for me to tell someone my name over the telephone.

I don't mean that it isn't easy.

I mean that it isn't possible.

Nothing I say, no sound I emit, can suffice to communicate to the person on the other end of the line what my name is. Even spelling it out only works if I make use of a conventionalized system for naming the letters (such as "Alpha, Lima, Victor, Alpha").

We confront what I will call the Paradox of Speech (a close cousin to Plato's Paradox of the Meno). To understand my words, you need already to know what I am saying. But if you already know what I am saying, there is no need to listen to my words.

How then is communication by speech even possible?

The solution to the paradox—understanding how speech is even possible—comes when we give up what we might have thought was a bedrock fact about language: the idea that speech is meaningful *sound*.

This won't come as a surprise to linguists. It has long been known that there is no one–one mapping between *physical* sound (acoustic phenomena picked out by spectral properties) and *speech* sound. The *k* you hear now and the *p* you hear later may be realized in identical acoustic events; and radically distinct acoustic events can be heard as one and the same speech sound.[1]

Does this mean that there is no difference between *pong* and *kong?* Is our conviction that these are different words somehow an illusion? Certainly not. But the difference isn't one we can make sense of in the vocabulary of physics. It isn't a difference in how these words *sound*.

If words aren't sounds, then what are they? One possibility— this is the idea I want to explore here—is that words are like home runs and that linguistic facts are like facts about baseball.

The rules of baseball tell you what a home run is, and they provide criteria for deciding, say, when a ball is foul. The rules of baseball jointly entail that there are unassisted triple plays but that there are no touchdowns.

To learn baseball is to learn much more than a system of rules, however. Players learn to field, run the bases, and hit. And whether you are a player or a fan, when you learn baseball, you acquire a whole suite of new perceptual skills. The botched double play, the right situation to put on a hit-and-run, the balk—these phenomena pop out for the knowledgeable observer. Even more remarkably, when you are initiated into the baseball world, you learn to *care* about such things as stolen bases and pickoff attempts. These things matter.

---

1. For a general discussion of this, D. W. Massaro's "Speech Perception," in James D. Wright (editor-in-chief), *International Encyclopedia of the Social & Behavioral Sciences, 2nd edition,* Vol 23. Oxford: Elsevier. pp. 235–242.

Far more than merely learning a system of rules, to learn baseball is to come to be able to see and feel and be motivated in ways that are meaningless to strangers of the game. Baseball is more than a system of rules; it is a practice.

Have you ever spent time with baseball people? If you have, then you know that the thing baseball folks do more than anything else, even during a game, is talk about baseball. I don't just mean that they dispute plays. Baseball people are endlessly engaged in evaluating plays and in developing theories—even mathematical and statistical theories—to justify or support one or another means of evaluation. They ask questions like, How much value does a player add to a team? Defensively? Offensively? And they ask the meta-question: By what methods can we decide such issues? Baseball people are concerned not just with how you play but also with the very question of how one ought to play baseball.

Let us say that a human social practice is *baseball-like* when the practice includes as a part of itself the activity of reflecting on, theorizing about, and critically evaluating the very practice itself. Baseball is baseball-like in this sense. And so are many, perhaps all, social practices. The law provides a clear example. But not everything is baseball-like. Digestion, for example, is not. However some people like to opine about how one ought to eat and how one ought not to eat to improve one's health and digestive performance, it remains the case that there is the first-order activity of digestion, and the second-order and distinct activity of talking and thinking about digestion. This sharp division into the first order and the second order, or into the practice and the ideologies about the practice, is not available to us when a practice is baseball-like.

What makes baseball-like practices interesting is the fact that, to put the point as a philosopher might, their ontologies are practice-relative. Are there home runs? *Of course*. But you can't look outside of the practice of baseball for an understanding of what home runs are. In particular, you can't turn to neuroscience, psychology, economics, biology, physics, or chemistry for such an explanation. A home run is, yes. But what is a home run? It is a structure in the space of baseball. A home run is a practical structure.

Let us turn our attention back to language. As with baseball, so with language. Language is a system of rules and representations, so the linguists like to say; but to learn a language is more than to learn rules.

It is to acquire a range of practical and perceptual skills, and it is to come to have a range of feelings, attitudes, and beliefs about language itself. Hearing speech is not just a matter of registering and categorizing sounds; this is what we noticed at the outset. It's also a way of paying attention to what people are doing—to what they say, to how they respond, to what they are paying attention to, and generally to what's going on.

A sensitivity to speech is, really, a sensitivity to human action.

And crucially, just as speech doesn't reduce to sound, action doesn't reduce to movement. I reach for the cup. One movement. But potentially multiple actions. In one case I am putting the cup away, let's say. In another case I am reaching to take a sip. These differences in action despite a sameness of movement are readily apparent.

From this standpoint we can appreciate that *of course* we can't hear novel words over the telephone. The very fact of their novelty removes the background context that makes perceptual sensitivity to the corresponding actions possible. What makes it possible to talk on the telephone is the fact that most of the time we can rely on the presence of a shared context or background. Everything flows smoothly until we get to the point where what I am doing now—articulating my unusual name, say—can't be read off the background we take for granted.

But most striking of all—in part because this runs against what linguists have been teaching for nearly a century—language is *baseball-like* in the sense defined earlier. To learn a language is to learn not just to do something but also to become all at once a critic, a teacher, and an innovator. Children don't merely learn what words mean. They learn to *ask* what words mean and, right away, to say what they mean, to tell or teach another, and they learn to correct and upbraid another for his or her usage.

The idea of a first-order linguistic practice that is unaffected by ideas about how one *ought* to speak is as strange and remote as the idea of a species of people who play baseball without ever talking or thinking about how one ought to play baseball. It would be a form of robot-like existence, certainly not a recognizably human one. Where there is understanding there is the possibility of misunderstanding. And clearing up misunderstandings belongs to the practice of communicating, too.

Linguistic science claims to be *descriptive* rather than *prescriptive*. Because linguistic performance itself is obviously the product of social forces and top-down prejudices, not to mention all manner of errors, slips of the tongue, and so on, what linguists seek to describe is not what people actually do and say but, as linguists put it, our underlying linguistic competence.

It is this competence that enables us to perceive, for example, that "every boy loves a person" is grammatical whereas "every boy love a person" is not. And it is this competence that allows us to understand, as it were unbiased by theory or ideology, that "a" and "person" go together in this previous sentence in a way that "loves" and "a" do not; they form a significant structural unit, a noun phrase.

Now it is surely the case that we are sensitive to these kinds of differences and these kinds of facts. But this is "inside baseball!" Asking about grammaticality, or how words group together, is like calling balls and strikes. We can do this. We can do this well. We can do it spontaneously. But we do this *within* the practice. "Grammatical" and "ungrammatical" are terms of appraisal; we deploy them within language, and they can't be used to demarcate the limits of language (any more than "witty" and "boring" could be so used). We are so deeply embedded within and at home in the language world (compare: the baseball world) that we find it difficult to believe in the practice relativity of our convictions and commitments.

Linguists insist that language and writing are very different. The latter is a 10,000-year-old bit of social technology. It is *obviously* baseball-like; the use of written language can't be separated from our attitudes about how one ought to write. But *language,* speech, real language—this is thought to be part of our species-specific genetic endowment; you can no more teach or correct language than you can teach or correct the growth of limbs or digestion.

I want to take seriously the possibility that the linguists have it wrong.

Language and writing are alike not merely in that both are baseball-like; their connection runs deeper than this. First, speech, like writing, is also a technology; or better, like writing, and baseball, it is a technique. Speech just happens to be older than writing by maybe 70,000 years. Second, writing has powerfully and utterly transformed our conception of language—so much so that we find it almost impossible to think of language other than in the terms afforded by writing; for example, we think of sentences as formal strings composed of a special kind of formal string, the word. But the idea that language is made up of formal strings, and that it can be studied as a system of rules governing the generation of formal strings, is about as plausible as the idea that dancing is a formal string that can be spelled and written and evaluated for its hidden structures.[2]

The deeper you go into physics and chemistry, the stranger the world gets. The objects of everyday life disappear. This is precisely not the case with linguistics. Linguistics begins with a pre-scientific conception of language as consisting in words and sentences (a conception *read off* of our use of writing to represent language). And it ends there, too.

What this reveals is not that there is anything suspect about the category of the word, or the sentence. What it reveals, rather, is that linguistics is not really in the business of uncovering hidden realities in the way that chemistry and physics are. The linguist uncovers, or helps us uncover, how we think about our practice.

---

2. I write about language and its relation to writing in "The Writerly Attitude," in *Symbolic Articulation: Image, Word, and Body Between Action and Schema*, edited by Sabine Marienberg (Boston: Walter de Gruyter, 2017), and also in *Strange Tools: Art and Human Nature* (New York: Farrar, Straus and Giroux, 2015), chapter 4.

But how we think about our practice is something we do inside the practice. We might say: the linguist works in the domain of style.

I once met a woman who was trilingual. She spoke Fulani at home, Hausa in the marketplace, and French at school and at the post office (and with me). She gave me the strangest look when I asked her how to translate a sentence from French to Fulani. It took me a long time to finally understand why she found the request strange. For her, the task of translating from French to Fulani was a bit like trying to understand how to do the twist in classical ballet, or how to score a touchdown in baseball. The request barely made sense and it had even less point. She implicitly understood, as I did not yet, that language is not an all-purpose symbolic system governed by rules and representations.

Language is like baseball.

11 | LINGUISTIC UNIVERSALS

The demands of communication put constraints on how everyone talks, regardless of what language they are using.

Imagine a race of beings who use language just like we do, but who never misunderstand each other; they never need to stop and ask for clarification, as language operates between them in a fluid way. Communication is like the flow of currents and they are all caught up in the flow.

This would be a little like imagining a race of baseball players who never made errors. Or perhaps it would be like imagining baseball players who never challenge or dispute calls. Not because they are stoic or disciplined and refuse to be distracted by thoughts about the game they are playing, but because they reside wholly and completely at the first-order level of play themselves; they live inside the game and never view it as an umpire or member of the audience might.

Baseball isn't like that. And language isn't, either. One of the first things kids learn when they learn to talk is to talk *about* talking. They ask what words mean. And they tell you what words mean. And they criticize you for using words wrong. It's not just that language—and baseball, too—is self-referential; it's of the essence of being a language user that you are also a language monitor.

Mark Dingemanse, of the Max Planck Institute for Psycholinguistics in Nijmegen, Netherlands, and Nick Enfield, of the University of Sydney, together with a large team of collaborators, have recently published a remarkable paper that sheds light on this phenomenon.[1]

When people talk—according to their survey of twelve languages spoken on five continents—they ask for clarification about every 90 seconds. *Huh? Who? She did what?* These devices for repairing communicative misfires saturate our conversational lives.

Indeed, beyond that, the researchers show that listeners will use the most specific—that is to say, the most precise—request for repair whenever they can. Instead of just saying "Huh?" whenever there is a misunderstanding, they drill down and ask "Who?" or "What?" or even the narrower "*Who* had a baby?" In other words, listeners work together with speakers; they collaborate to facilitate communication.

In recent years, it has become common among linguists to suppose that there are semantic and syntactic universals underlying the apparent variety of human languages. These shared features of language are often explained as belonging to an innate universal grammar.

Dingemanse and Enfield have uncovered a whole other kind of linguistic universal. These "pragmatic" or "conversational" universals are constraints placed on linguistic variation by the

---

1. Mark Dingemanse, Nick Enfield, et al., "Universal Principles in the Repair of Communication Problems," *PLOS One*, September 16, 2015, https://doi.org/10.1371/journal.pone.013610; 0.

conditions of language use and, in particular, by the demands of being social.

Language isn't just an assignment of "semantic values" to strings of sounds. As they remind us, the "ecological niche" of language is conversation, and conversation would be impossible—nonadaptive—if it didn't contain the resources for coping with communicative breakdown. It is the shared fact that we live and work and communicate together that grounds these linguistic universals and not, as is sometimes claimed about syntactic or semantic ones, facts about language as an innate competence.

Their extraordinary claim is that this fact alone—that human communication requires the ability to correct misunderstanding in real time during conversation—has led to a cross-cultural convergence not only on specific strategies for repair but also, in some cases, even on shared words. "Huh?," they have also argued, is a universal word.[2]

Consider: the word for milk in German is *Milch*. In French it is *lait*. Two quite different words—*Milch, lait*—to refer to one thing. This is the basic observation that supports the linguistic principle that the relation between words and their meanings is arbitrary. You can't read the meaning off the word. And what a word means doesn't determine or shape the word itself. The bottom line: you need to learn words.

And that's why you don't find the same words in every language. Sameness of word implies a shared history. No shared

2. Mark Dingemanse, F. Torreira, and Nick J. Enfield, "Is 'Huh?' a Universal Word? Conversational Infrastructure and the Convergent Evolution of Linguistic Items," *PLOS One*, November 8, 2013, https://doi.org/10.1371/journal.pone.0078273.

history, no shared words. English and German share the word for milk (German *Milch*), but that's because German and English share a common history. And there are words like "OK" that have pretty wide circulation but only thanks to globalization and the influence of English.

It would be astonishing if there was a word—or a group of words—that was actually native to *all* languages. This is precisely the claim made by Dingemanse and his colleagues. "Huh?"—as in, "huh? what did you say?"—it is claimed, is a universal word. It occurs in every language (or in some suitably large sample of unrelated languages).

They do not claim "Huh?" occurs in exactly the same form in all languages. Think *Milch* and "milk." A certain amount of variation is consistent with word identity, not only across languages but also within language. Some English speakers say "mulk," others "melk," and so on. And so for this case. When it comes to "Huh?" there are other kinds of differences, too. It's a *question word*, and different languages use different prosody to mark the interrogative mood (e.g., some languages, like English, use rising intonation, whereas others, like Icelandic, use falling).

Exactly *how* "Huh?" gets said varies from language to language.

Which turns out to be a crucial, for it rules out a natural objection to the claim of universality. "Huh?" is universal, you could argue, because it isn't a word! It isn't the sort of sound that needs to be learned. You don't need to learn to sneeze, or grunt. You don't need to learn to jump when you are startled. "Huh?" must be like this.

But you do need to learn to say "Huh?" in just the ways we need to learn the word for milk and ask questions. "Huh?" is not only universal, like sneezing, it is also a word, like "milk."

This brings us to the central puzzle the authors face: given that you need to learn words, and that meanings don't fix the sound, shape, or character of the words we use to express them, and given that linguistic cultures are diverse and unrelated, how could there be universal words?

The authors' proposal is startling. I reserve judgment on whether it's right or not.

Their basic claim, already hinted at above, is that this is an example of what in biology is called *convergent evolution*. Sometimes lineages that are unrelated evolve the same traits as adaptations to the same environmental conditions. Evolution in cases such as this *converges*. And that, according to the authors, is what's going on here. It turns out that every language faces the "Huh?" problem. That is, every language needs a way for a listener to signal to the speaker that the message has not been received. (Every language needs what the authors call a mechanism for "Other-Initiated Repair.") Why? Because, as we have considered, where there is communication there is liable to be miscommunication. Just as the risk of missing balls comes with playing catch, so too the possibility of not hearing, or not understanding what you hear, not getting it, comes with speech. Where there is speech you need a way to say: Huh?

Their bold claim is that only interjections that sound roughly like "Huh?" can do this. "Huh?" is optimal—it's short, easy to produce, easy to hear, capable of carrying a questioning tone, and so on—and it is for this reason that every human language has stumbled upon *it* as a solution.

This ability to pause conversation and fix it on the fly is, they suggest, unique to human language. We humans don't just talk, just as we don't just mechanically bang a ball back and forth when we play ball. It seems to be our special genius as a species, or perhaps our curse, not just to go with the flow but also to cope with what happens when our flow is interrupted, as it inevitably is.

Baseball exhibits a similar language-like concern, not so much with self-repair as with self-representation. To play ball is to allow oneself to be preoccupied with the question just what it is that one is doing.

Hmm.

12 | THE COMMUNICATION GAME

I was sitting with my six-year-old son on the train in Berlin. We'd only just arrived in Germany and my son, as of yet, knew no German. Across from us sat a man reading the newspaper. On the seat next to him, sitting for all the world like a passenger, was the man's dog. That sight alone was amusing to us. My son leaned over and said to the man, in English, "Is your dog friendly?" The man looked at my boy with confusion. "Is your dog friendly?" my son repeated. In response he received a blank stare of confusion. I then said, in German, "Ist er freundlich?" At those familiar words in the man's native German, his brow cleared and he turned to us and said, in perfect English, "Indeed, he is most friendly!" And he added, in English, "I must be going deaf!"[1]

Scholars of language like to say that language is a complicated symbolic system. To know a language is to know the rules that regulate how we can combine words, with their meanings, into more complex expressions we call sentences. Talking is encoding meaning in sound in this way, and understanding is the act of

---

1. This paragraph is adapted from my *Out of Our Heads: Why You Are Not Your Brain And Other Lessons from the Biology of Consciousness* (New York: Farrar, Straus and Giroux, 2009).

decoding. To talk is to manipulate the events in another person's mind by presenting them with encoded ideas in sound form.

But this S-Bahn example doesn't fit this picture at all. Why couldn't the man *hear* what my son was saying? The man could hear the sounds, but not the speech, and it was only when he knew the meaning that he could hear the speech.

In chapters 10 and 11, I argued that baseball provides insight into the nature of language. I return to this theme here. Baseball can help us understand what happened that morning on the S-Bahn.

Surely one of the most remarkable things about baseball is that it is structured around a series of one-on-one encounters between the pitcher and the batter. And it is the internal structure of the *at-bat*—you could write whole books about single at-bats—that defines the game.[2] From the standpoint of the at-bat, it is only the pitcher and the batter that matter. Everyone else is supporting cast.

The batter's task during an at-bat is simple to understand but difficult to execute. Niceties aside, he wants to get a hit. Because the balls come at him so fast, his only real hope of getting a hit is to anticipate what the pitcher will throw. This task is easier than you might think—although it isn't easy—because what the pitcher is likely to throw is constrained in comprehensible ways by a number of factors, such as what he *can* throw, what he *has* thrown, what the count is (i.e., whether he or the batter has the advantage), whether there are men on base, and so on. What's critical is that batters

---

2. Keith Hernandez, the former Mets and Cardinals great, has in fact written a captivating book-length, pitch-by-pitch analysis of two complete baseball games. Keith Hernandez and Mike Bryan, *Pure Baseball: Pitch by Pitch for the Advanced Fan* (New York: HarperCollins, 1994).

have no need to stand at the ready for *any possible* pitch, no more than chess players need to consider *all possible* moves. Context limits possibilities, in chess and in baseball, to a manageable few. Given the rationality and competence of your opponent, you can be pretty sure he'll select his pitch from among a small group of options.

Now let's turn to the pitcher. His task during an at-bat is not only difficult to execute but almost impossible to understand. Frankly, it's absurd. It would be *easy* to throw balls that the batter can't hit. You could lob balls over his head, or bounce them along the ground, or throw them behind him. But you are not allowed to do that. If you do that, the batter gets a free base. No, you are required to throw him balls that he can hit. But you are to do so without letting him hit them! So your job, basically, is to throw him hittable balls he can't hit. Ouch! The poet Robert Francis puts it well: the pitcher's aim is "how not to hit the mark he seems to aim at." He must "avoid the obvious," and to do this he learns "to vary the avoidance."

As a pitcher, your arsenal is the pitches themselves, balls that come at the batter so fast or that curve or break in such devilishly surprising ways that even though the balls are right there, in reach, in the strike zone, they are unhittable. The problem is, the batters are professionals. They already know your pitches; they've studied your films, they've hit against you before, they are coached. So your biggest weapon, really, is surprise. For example, with the count in the batter's favor, you know that he knows that you know that you need to throw a strike, and you guess that he'll guess that you'll go for your best pitch, your put-away pitch, the fastball. So you throw something else and see if you can cross him up.

The at-bat, then, is a delicate *conversation.* It is an exchange or transaction that can only take place against the background of the game. And of course *the game* here is a situation that is defined not primarily in terms of velocities and vectors and reaction times but, rather, in terms of expectations about shared understandings, known objectives, and a common appreciation of what is fair and acceptable conduct.

And so with language. The man on the train wasn't going deaf! He couldn't perceive my son's words because he was unable, in that context and at that early hour of the morning, to find anything remotely intelligible about the sounds my son was making. I don't think the fact that my son's English was that of a six-year-old was particularly a factor. The man knew English, but he didn't expect English in that situation, and so he was as good as deaf. It was as if my son had tossed him a baseball as he sat there. He might be able to catch perfectly well. But it was only when he clicked that my son was playing the English-language conversation game with him that it was also possible for him to understand.

We don't hear sounds and assign arbitrary meanings to them when we talk. We play ball.

13 | A MOMENT MISUNDERSTOOD

We see and hear what we expect to see and hear, at least a fair bit of the time. I don't have to actually hear your response to my "How are you?" to be pretty sure what you said in reply.

And it is striking that, as the linguist Geoffrey Pullum once mentioned to me, if I mention my *hat*, and then my *scarf* and then go on to mention my *dloves*, you will very certainly hear what context dictates I am likely to have said—which is not *dloves* (not only is that not a word in English but the *dl* sound doesn't even exist in English) but, of course, *gloves*.

This isn't necessarily a bad thing. It lets us hear and make sense of each other even when conditions are suboptimal or words are slurred or in some other way garbled. And anyway, we're not interested in the sounds we make, but in what we are saying. And context goes a long way toward shaping that.

We can see this basic fact about human perception working itself out in baseball.

Baseball players, like other athletes endowed with extraordinary sensory-motor skills, don't necessarily always have faster reflexes or better vision than the rest of us. If hitting a fastball or returning a serve were dependent on reaction times, then, well, it'd be impossible to do either. The familiar advice of the coach to

89

keep your eye on the ball is not something it is possible for a hitter to follow. The third of a second or less that is available just isn't enough time to see, to decide, and to act.

The good news is that we don't need to do the impossible. As in conversations, batters often have a good idea, much better than a guess, what a pitcher is going to throw. Not every pitcher can throw any pitch, and not any pitch would be appropriate in any situation. What batters excel at, generally, is reading the intention and body language of the pitcher against the background of their understanding of the situation.

What marks expert athletes from novices, as Janet Starkes of McMaster University showed in the 1980s, is not their special physiology or reaction times but, rather, their ability to take in the meaning or significance of a situation right away.[1] Novices need to figure things out. William Chase and Herbert Simon had demonstrated a similar finding about chess players.[2] They are not better at remembering arbitrary arrangements of pieces on boards. But they are *very* good at remembering possible chess positions. For these aren't merely arrangements of pieces on boards, they are *milieu*; that is to say, they are meaningful situations in which one side is on the attack and the other is vulnerable, or in which forces are awkwardly balanced, or whatever.

---

1. See Janet L. Starkes and K. Anders Ericsson, *Expert Performance in Sports: Advances in Research on Sports Expertise* (Windsor, Ontario: Human Kinetics, 2003).
2. William Chase and Herbert Simon, "Perception in Chess," *Cognitive Psychology* (1973): 55–81.

We remember meaning. We understand organization. In baseball, meaning isn't a matter of brute physics; just as in speech, it isn't a matter of the sounds you produce.

About ten years ago, superstar women's fast-pitch softball pitcher Jennie Finch went on the road to challenge baseball's best hitters to try their luck batting against her. Hurling softballs against MLB superstars—Albert Pujols and future Hall of Famer Mike Piazza, for example—Finch made the very best baseball hitters of the day look like amateurs. They couldn't touch her.[3]

How can we explain this? It's true that a fastball thrown at 95 mph from a mound 60 feet, 6 inches away arrives 40 or some odd milliseconds *later* than Finch's underarm 70-mph pitch, tossed from 43 feet away.

But guys like Pujols routinely hit balls thrown a lot faster than 95 mph. What explains their inability to make any contact at all with a larger, green softball?

The interesting story here isn't about baseball versus softball, nor is it a battle of the sexes. No, the interesting story here—and why it remains relevant—is what it reveals about expertise and action.

The baseball players couldn't hit Finch's balls, not because she was too fast, or they were too slow, or because of her distinctive angle of attack. It wasn't physics that made her balls unhittable. What made her pitches impossible to hit was that she was, in a word, *strange*. She was serving *dlove* when all they knew was *glove*.

---

3. For a nice discussion of the case of Jennie Finch, see David Epstein's *The Sports Gene: Inside the Science of Extraordinary Athletic Performance* (New York: Current/Penguin Group, 2014).

She was speaking a language they didn't understand. Which isn't surprising. She isn't a baseball player; she plays a different game.

What makes hitting, like any other form of communication, possible is our participation together in an ongoing game or play or, better, relationship. Again, the poet Robert Francis nails it: whereas the others throw to be comprehended, the pitcher throws to be a moment misunderstood. The pitcher lets the batter understand *too late*.

14 | NOBODY'S PERFECT

In the baseball world, there are two distinct theories of umpiring.

Some view umpires as, in essence, instruments, somewhat outdated, for measuring baseball facts. From this standpoint, every "bad call" is an occasion to demand improvements in measurement technology. Umpires call them as they see them, but they don't see any better than the rest of us. They should be eliminated by, or at least supplemented with, instant replay and other new measuring devices.

Others, however, think of umpires as, in effect, a special class of player in the game; they are no less a part of the game than the players themselves. From this standpoint, the demand that we replace umpires with machines has about as much to recommend it as the idea that one might remove or replace the players themselves to improve the game. It's an idiotic idea.

These two distinct ideas about umpiring correspond to what are really distinct philosophies of the game. Corresponding to the umpire-as-instrument idea is Realism. According to Realism, there are umpiring-independent facts of the game—balls really are fair or foul, runners are either safe or out—and the questions we face are merely *epistemological*: how best to determine the facts, how to find out.

Corresponding to the umpire-as-player idea is Anti-Realism. According to Anti-Realism, umpires don't call them as they see them; umpires, through their calls, *make it the case* that a pitch is a strike or a ball, a runner is safe or out. There are no umpire-independent facts in baseball.

Realism does a good job accounting for the apparent fact that there are "bad calls" and also the fact that dispute and controversy seem to be ever-present parts of the game. After all, it is facts of the matter about, say, whether someone is safe or out, that grounds the possibility that umpires can be mistaken. Anti-Realism, for its part, is helpless to make sense of this. If what an umpire says goes, then how can we even take seriously the idea that an umpire might be mistaken?

But Anti-Realism gets something right, too. Baseball facts are not like facts of physics. Consider: what interests us in baseball is whether players succeed or fail, whether they achieve or get lucky. The judgment that a ball is a strike is, from the Anti-Realist standpoint, the judgment that a pitcher delivered a pitch that the batter *ought* to have hit. This is not so much a judgment about where the pitch was located as it is a judgment about whether the pitcher or the batter deserves credit. It is, in the original sense of the term, and as I have already explained, a forensic judgment. It is, therefore, a decision made within the context of the game, with its distinct interests, problems, and dynamics in mind. Thought of in these terms, umpiring—together with official scoring—is an ineliminable part of the sport. Realism seems helpless to account for this forensic side of baseball.

Realism and Anti-Realism are extremist views. A better view—let's call it Internal Realism—agrees with Anti-Realism that there are no baseball facts apart from the internal standpoint of the game. There is no merely physical, practice-independent conception of what a "fair ball," a "home run," or a "strike" even is. These are events that only exist inside baseball.[1]

At the same time, Internal Realism acknowledges that there can be legitimate disputes about whether a runner was really out, or whether a ball was in the strike zone, as Realism had maintained. Crucially, however, according to the Internal Realist, you don't need to step outside of the practice and take up "a view from the outside" to call plays in baseball. A concern for whether a call was correctly made is something we do precisely from the inside. These questions have the significance they do because we are *interested* in the game, because we are participants.

From the standpoint of the Internal Realist, of course it is legitimate to question an umpire's call. The Realist is right about that. There are facts of the matter. But, the Internal Realist insists, these are facts that only come into focus *within* baseball, and the disputes themselves, no less than mundane unchallenged calls, are baseball events. Disputing plays does not force us outside baseball, beyond its boundaries; they happen on the field of play and belong to the game itself.[2]

---

1. Internal Realism is an idea that originates in and was central to the work of Hilary Putnam. See, for example, his *Reason, Truth and History* (Cambridge: Cambridge University Press, 1981).

2. The philosopher Robert Brandom (in *Making It Explicit: Reasoning, Representing and Discursive Commitment* (Cambridge, MA: Harvard University Press, 1994) refers to an old joke about three umpires. The first says: "I calls 'em as I sees 'em." The second says: "I calls 'em as they is." The third says: "Until I calls 'em, they ain't." Brandom takes this up because he's concerned to understand how any such view of the umpire's calls as

If we advocate Internal Realism, we get the advantages of Realism and Anti-Realism, without any of their disadvantages.

But let us ask: If we adopt this improved standpoint, what should we say about calls for changes in umpiring, for the introduction of instant replay, or computerized ball and strike measurement?

This is a hard question to answer, in part because we can reasonably wonder whether *this* question about the reform of baseball practices is itself an internal or an external question. Insofar as the Internal Realist is a *Realist,* then we must acknowledge that the outcome of disputes matters. But insofar as we are *Anti-Realist*, then we must acknowledge that to change the basic character of the baseball practice is, really, to change what it is for something to be a ball or a strike, a fair or foul ball; it is to shift and transform baseball reality.

What would, or could, count as a reason for doing this?

Back in 2010, Armando Galarraga was one out away from pitching a rare perfect game, a game in which no opposing player managed to reach base. A "bad call" at first base by umpire James Joyce robbed him of his deserved glory. Joyce admitted this after the game and, in a wildly unprecedented move, he apologized to Galarraga. The latter accepted the apology with grace and humility and is reported to have said: "Nobody's perfect."

"making it the case" that a ball is a strike or that a runner is fair can ever be subject to challenge. How can it even make sense to think an umpire might be wrong? Brandom, who is responding to a paper by David Lewis called "Scorekeeping in a Language Game" (*Journal of Philosophical Logic* 8, no. 3 (1979): 339–359), is interested in the broader question how can we think critically or reflectively, from the outside, as it were, about the very rules and principles that help constitute what it is to think in the first place.

Making Peace with Our Cyborg Nature

15 | "THE POSITIVE ROLE OF MEDICINE IN OUR GAME'S GROWTH"

The very same week that Ryan Braun—known lovingly to his fans in Milwaukee as the Hebrew Hammer—was suspended for testing positive for performance-enhancing drugs (PEDs), the Baseball Hall of Fame, during its annual induction ceremonies in Cooperstown, New York, celebrated the life and accomplishments of Frank Jobe. It is hard not to be impressed by the irony of this.

Who is Frank Jobe and what is his contribution to the sport of baseball? Jobe is the inventor of ulnar collateral ligament (UCL) reconstruction, known widely as Tommy John surgery (after its first patient).

The background: Pitching is bad for you. The act of pitching tears shoulder capsules and destroys elbow ligaments. Pain is a pitcher's bedfellow. Just call to mind the iconic photograph of Sandy Koufax with his left arm in a bucket of ice after a game. Tommy John himself tells how the pain in his pitching arm began when he was thirteen years old!

If you want to pitch, you learn to live with it.

Success as a pitcher has always been a battle with pain and a race against time. When the pain is too great, it's time to stop. Many pitchers need to hang up their cleats before they get started, still in high school or in the minor leagues. For others, the end of the line comes later.

Enter Frank Jobe: he developed a way not merely to mitigate injury but also completely to undo the effects of years of damage to the ligaments in the elbow. Tommy John surgery allows pitchers not merely to extend their careers but also to have careers that by all genetic rights they never should have had. John himself went on to pitch for another *fourteen years* after what would have been the career-stopping blowout of his elbow. It is now commonplace for pitchers to undergo Tommy John surgery *at the start* of their careers. About 500 major leaguers have had Tommy John. It is impossible to say how many children, minor leaguers, and college athletes have undergone the expensive procedure.

Why was Frank Jobe being honored at the Baseball Hall of Fame? The answer is simple: he can be credited with having changed the game. He did that by utterly reshaping the career of the pitcher. From the Hall of Fame press release:

> The ground-breaking work of Dr. Frank Jobe to conceptualize, develop, refine and make mainstream Tommy John Surgery, a complex elbow procedure that has furthered the careers of hundreds of ballplayers, is a testament to the positive role of medicine in our game's growth. . . .

"The positive role of medicine in our game's growth."

That sounds about right. Jobe deserved the honor he was receiving. Baseball players and fans are and should be grateful.

But now we come to the source of the irony I mentioned: Why do we view the use of Jobe's particular brand of artificial, performance-altering technology as exemplary of the positive role medicine plays in baseball, but we view the use of other kinds of medical technologies—performance-enhancing *medicines*—as somehow anathema?

Don't surgery and the medicines have broadly the same effects—that of enabling athletes to play better longer, to manage pain, and to recover from injury?

Why are drugs bad when surgery is just fine?

True, PEDs have been banned. So it's cheating to use them. Not so surgery. Sports surgery is permitted.

But this just begs the issue. *Why* have we banned use of performance-enhancing medicine but not performance-enhancing surgery? Why do we salute the surgeons and vilify the pharmacists?

And let's not forget that we tend to discount the achievements of athletes who used PEDs even before these substances were banned. Drug use in baseball isn't thought of as bad because it is banned. We banned the use of drugs because we think it is bad. And so the question is: What's so bad about it? Why is it cheating to take medicines that help your body cope with exhaustion and wear and tear, but it's not cheating to pay someone to rebuild your entire elbow?

Nor is it any help to be reminded that the use of PEDs is a risky business.

So is surgery!

And anyway, the use of PEDs would be much less dangerous if they were to be administered, as with surgery, under a doctor's supervision.

You might argue that PEDs alter play, allowing athletes to reach unnatural heights. Tommy John surgery, in contrast, just extends the life of a player.

But this doesn't withstand scrutiny. You can count on *one* hand the number of pitchers who have thrown more than 700 games, won more than 285, pitched more than 160 complete games, gotten more than 2,200 strikeouts, and thrown more than 4,600 innings. And Tommy John is one of them. But only thanks to the surgery.

Or consider the case of a pitcher like Jenrry Mejia. The Mets drafted him when he was sixteen; he blew out his elbow when he was twenty-two. Tommy John surgery gave him a second chance. The Mets had high hopes for him, largely, we now know, on the strength of his youthful use of performance-enhancing surgical modifications of his body. Those hopes were dashed when Mejia was suspended for using PEDS, first once, then twice, and then a third time, earning him in 2016 the distinct honor of being the first MLB pitcher to be handed a lifetime ban from the sport. He was banned for using performance-enhancing medicines when it was only thanks to performance-enhancing surgery that he even had a shot at a life in baseball in the first place. Is there a justifiable rationale here?

Sure, the use of surgery has transformed the game and made possible new kinds of achievement. This is why the Hall of Fame honored Jobe, after all.

So we are thrown back on our question: What explains our positive view of the place of surgery in baseball when we think of medicine as such a destructive presence?

I can't say for sure, but here's a hypothesis. It has nothing to do with cheating but everything to do with the way we, in our culture, or at least in certain segments of our culture, think about ourselves, about what it is to be human.

Despite the fact that surgeons go inside your body and rebuild parts and structures, we think of them as leaving *you* basically unaffected. Surgeons don't change your being any more than plumbers change architecture. Surgery is superficial.

But when it comes to drugs, an entirely different set of intuitions kick in. Drugs, we think, are not superficial. Drugs get inside you in a deeper way; drugs change you. What you do under the influence of drugs—well, that's not your doing. It's the drug's doing. And so we find ourselves inclined to think that if you need drugs to be a good athlete—or if you need drugs to be happy or live without anxiety or perform sexually—then, well, you are not really a good athlete (or a happy person or a good lover). Drugs make a person inauthentic.

Now if I am right, as I have been arguing throughout this book, that baseball is a forensic sport—that is, that baseball is a game whose play itself consists, in good measure, in finding ways to assign praise and blame—then it is easy to appreciate that drugs pose a special problem for baseball. Baseball is an agency game. And drug use undercuts legitimate assignments of agency.

Of course, this is so only if it is true that drugs, but not surgery, or a good upbringing, or all the other advantages and enablers that contribute to a life in baseball, or simply to a life, somehow distinctively undercut our claims to agency, our ownership of our own achievements.

Do they? Is this true? To answer this, we need to think less about baseball, sports in general, or principles of fair play, and more about how we, in this society, comprehend what it is to be a human being.

16 | MAKING PEACE WITH OUR CYBORG NATURE

I loved the TV show *The Six Million Dollar man* when I was growing up. For me, Steve Austin (played by Lee Majors) wasn't less cool because he had bionic implants that enabled him to perform superhuman feats. He was more cool.

For millions of years, our ancestors survived with only the crudest implements. Some 35,000 to 75,000 years ago, a technological revolution took place on an extraordinary scale. Innovation now abounds in the archeological record. Whereas before, generation after generation used the same blunt pounding tools, now we find highly refined instruments for cutting. And we find tools for making tools. We find an increased diversity of building materials and evidence of real specialization in tool use and tool manufacture. We can also date back to this time the emergence of graphic art, clothing, and, we speculate, language.

What explains this burst of technological progress? Did we get smarter? Or did denser populations, trade, and other changes in our mode of living make it possible, for the first time, to build on the innovations of previous generations?

However we answer these questions, this much is clear: the appearance of cognitively modern human beings is coeval with the integration into human living of the innovative and productive use of tools. We are truly the tool-using species, not because we are the only species to use tools but because the use of tools is essential to what we are. Tools organize us.

We see this everywhere we look. You can only frame a thought about a negative integer thanks to the availability of our shared notational tools. Science, art, law, politics—can we imagine any of this without writing? Can we imagine *ourselves* in the absence of all this? The simple answer is that we cannot.

We like to think that here is the person and there are the tools he or she uses to solve this or that problem. But, in fact, the tools are internal to the kinds of lives we live, and so to the kinds of problems we face. If we lacked shoes and cars and planes, we couldn't carry on the kinds of projects that we do. We wouldn't be the kind of people we are.

Or, think of the way that communication technology organizes a workplace. Remove the communication technology—phones, email, social networking software—and you don't have the same organization minus the technology. You have something organized differently, or maybe something disorganized.

Whether we think of knowledge, or communication, or perception, or medicine, or commerce, or the arts, we live in a vast web of organized human exchanges and shared practices. We are technologists by nature. Or to use philosopher Andy Clark's apt phrase, we are "natural-born cyborgs."[1]

---

1. See Clark's book by the same name: *Natural-Born Cyborgs: Minds, Technologies and the Future of Human Intelligence* (New York: Oxford University Press, 2004). For a

The point is not just that we couldn't do what we do without tools. The point is that we couldn't think what we think or see what we see without tools. We wouldn't be what we are without tools. Making tools, and changing tools, is a way of making new ways of being. Technologies are evolving patterns of human organization.

Consider: we are animals who can digest milk. But only because we first domesticated milk-bearing animals. When we did that, just a few thousand years ago, we in effect genetically engineered ourselves!

Let us turn then to the case of the disgraced cycling giant Lance Armstrong. He didn't win races on his own. No, he created an organization, one drawing on other people and on the creative and effective use of technology, the mastery of biochemistry, and he deployed this to enable him to go places and do things that most of us never will, and that no one ever had before him. This makes him one of the greats. A trailblazer.

That we attack him, that we tear him down, that we minimize his achievements—what does this tell us about ourselves? Perhaps this: that we are in conflict about our nature as human beings. We fantasize that we are something—self-contained, autonomous, heroic, islands unto ourselves—that we are not. The doping athlete is an affront because he or she conforms to a truth about ourselves that we would deny.[2]

---

related and early appreciation of the cyborg-nature of human being, see Donna Haroway's *Simians, Cyborgs and Women: The Reinvention of Nature* (New York: Routledge, 1991).

2. I investigate this idea that tools are modes of social organization that make us what we are in *Strange Tools: Art and Human Nature* (New York: Farrar, Straus and Giroux, 2015).

17 | PLAGIARIZED PERFORMANCE

Are all four of a horse's hooves off the ground at the same time when it gallops?

They say the answer to this question was not known before Eadweard Muybridge's pioneering work in stop-motion photography in the 1870s. It doesn't surprise me that painters might have inaccurately depicted the galloping horse, but I find it almost impossible to believe that people working closely with horses—cowboys, cavalry officers, dressage competitors—would not have known the answer to this question.

I thought of this recently when I learned that some sports teams are now using new motion-capture technologies—of the sort used, for example, in the making of computer-animated films—to help train athletes.[1] The idea is that by constructing accurate 3D models of a given athlete's motion, they can help him, or her, avoid injury, speed up recovery, and, in general, optimize overall performance. Some baseball teams, according to the article, have secret programs in this area in the hope that they can get a competitive edge.

---

1. James Glanz and Alan Schwarz, "From 'Avatar' Playbook, Athletes Use 3-D Imaging," *New York Times,* October 2, 2010.

I want to pose a question here that may at first strike you as silly. Why is this sort of use of technology any better than, or in principle any different from, the use by athletes of steroids (or other so-called performance-enhancing drugs)? The goals are certainly the same: to avoid injury, to speed up recovery, to optimize performance, to gain a competitive edge.

Many people have a strong conviction that drug use in sports is bad; that it is bad in a special way. Is it really?

Well, you might say, doping is prohibited in most sports (professional and amateur). It's cheating to use a banned substance. End of story.

Granted.

But this actually begs the issue (that is, it presupposes a stand on precisely what we are trying to figure out). The question is not: Are they banned? The question is: Ought they to be banned? Presumably, steroids in sports are not bad *because* they are banned. They are banned because they are bad. And the question is, Why?

One answer goes like this: "Steroids and other performance-enhancing drugs are *harmful*! They destroy your body. We reserve a special contempt for drug use in sports because sports celebrates the beauty, grace, and power of the healthy, trained body. Doping kills."

This statement is clear and to the point. But it isn't persuasive.

Steroids may be dangerous. But almost everything about sports, at both professional and amateur levels, is dangerous. Athletes pay a very high price to do what they do. It isn't trivial to find a professional athlete in his or her forties who has *not* had multiple surgeries to repair serious damage to the knees or hips or shoulders! And the list doesn't stop there. Concussion, premature arthritis, chronic pain, even premature death—this is the lot of the *successful* athlete. It's hard to see how steroid use, or the use of other drugs to improve performance, changes the equation.

I grant that the use of banned substances in sports is disturbing. The image of MLB players shooting each other up in toilet stalls is appalling. But what if teams had drug specialists as part of their training programs, just as teams now, reportedly, have digital motion-capture graphics specialists on the payroll? Under the right conditions—that is, with the right kind of research support and medical supervision—use of drugs by athletes might actually *improve* their health and safety by, for example, helping their bodies cope better with the extraordinarily brutal wear and tear of their labor.

Would we stand back from our opposition to drugs in sports if we could find a way to make them safe for the athletes, if we found that they actually improved the lives of athletes?

I think I hear you shouting (as you jump up and down): *But what about the children! Do we want to send our kids the message that to play sports at a competitive level they need to do drugs?*

To this I say, let's not lie to our kids or ourselves. A life in sports is a lot like a life in the military. You join a club. You get gear and a uniform. You have the chance to learn, travel, grow. You run the risk of getting maimed or otherwise injured.

Don't get me wrong. I love sports. But sports, like life, requires sacrifice.

The ideal of the noble amateur, like that of the Renaissance man, is long dead, if it ever really existed. And forget about *sound mind in sound body*. Sports is a jealous mistress and demands full commitment and specialization. And hip-replacement surgery before age forty and early onset dementia as a result of head trauma among football players are for real. If we aren't squeamish about surgery and dementia, why are we squeamish about doping?

So let's ask ourselves again: What is it about drug use in sports that seems so instinctively repellent—more repellent than the pain and the limping and the surgeries? Why the deep moral disapprobation? Why the outrage?

Here's a suggestion. We think of drug use in sports as a kind of plagiarism. We don't view an athlete's performance under conditions of drug use as authentically *his* or *her* performance.

When an athlete trains, we think he improves himself, and we think that his performance flows from and gives truthful expression to this improved self. When an athlete works with scientists and uses imaging and modeling technologies to improve his performance, we think that he gains knowledge, and we believe that this knowledge enhances him as a person and as an athlete, and so we believe that he has achieved his improved performance and he deserves our admiration.

But when an athlete takes drugs, we feel, he does not so much enhance himself as he becomes an imposter of himself. An athlete on drugs has made himself an unnatural creature, a cyborg, a monster. The very being of such a person, we feel, is a cheat.

So the outrage that many people feel when Barry Bonds is credited with being the "Home Run King" stems not from the fact that he had a supposedly unfair advantage when compared to Babe Ruth or Hank Aaron. No, the source of the outrage is the feeling that Barry Bonds didn't really do what he claims to have done. He didn't hit those home runs. He faked it, or he hit *sham* home runs. To reward him for his accomplishments is like rewarding a person for having assembled a stamp collection when, in fact, he inherited it.

Now consider this: Barry Bonds's home runs are in fact not like breast implants. You pay for the latter, and the surgeon does the work. The home runs, however, are not simply purchased for the price of taking the medicine. The drugs only bring about their desired effects when integrated intelligently into the training regimen and practice of the skilled athlete. Bonds was one of the greatest athletes ever to play the game of baseball, and that fact has nothing to do with alleged steroid use. It was his greatness that let him parlay (alleged) steroid use into such unmatched achievements.

Performance-enhancing drugs are best compared with performance-enhancing footwear, or bathing suits, or training techniques. They are a tool in the arsenal of the competitor. They do not suffice, on their own, for excellent performance in the way that the plastic surgeon's work, all on its own, suffices for breast enlargement.

Our sense that drugs make a sham of what we accomplish, whereas bathing suits and training regimens simply enable our enhanced performance, is without justification. There is no sharp line to be drawn between myself, say, and what I can do, on the one hand, and my environment and what it allows and affords me, on the other. This is because, in general, there is no sharp line to be drawn between mechanisms and their enabling conditions.

Pills, like meals, sneakers, and bathing caps, are on a par—they are tools. And like all tools, they hold out the possibility of expanding not only our bodies but also our selves (as well as the possibility of being abused or misused).

For the record: I am not in support of doping. A strong case can be made that the quality of play in baseball has improved overall since the stricter enforcement of the drugs ban. And I grant that, since the ban, it is straightforward that cheats need to be punished.

But what motivates me here is the conviction that underlying our moralizing and outrage in the face of drugs in baseball and other sports is an unreflected upon and ultimately implausible conception of the self as the entirely internal, self-sufficient source of outflowing action.

The problem with this romantic conception of ourselves as islands of self-determination is that it isn't believable.[2] We are all technologically enhanced. In a way, we are all cyborg-like monsters. Perhaps you wear contact lenses, consume vitamins and antidepressants, or enjoy the benefits of fancy dental work. But what are these technologies other than tools for enhancing performance in daily life? Even the food we eat is the result of thousands of years of agricultural engineering. The more recent advent of genetically modified crops amplifies this ancient and enduring fact.

Tools and equipment—the dwellings we live in, the clothes we wear, the cars we move around in—are prosthetic extensions of ourselves. We don't use them merely to achieve familiar goals. Our use of tools radically changes us. Monkeys using rakes have been shown to have enlarged cortical representations of their hands and arms. But it isn't only our bodies that extend into and get made up out of the world around us. The same is true of our minds. We can

2. This is one of the themes of my book *Out of Our Heads: Why You Are Not Your Brain and Other Lessons from the Biology of Consciousness* (New York: Farrar, Straus and Giroux, 2009).

think about prime numbers and places we've never been because we deploy language and other shared, evolved symbolic systems to do so. We "know how to find our way" by relying on landmarks, signs, maps, and GPS systems. We keep track of the time on our wrists. Each of us is the product of a genetic endowment and a lived history. What is an education but the R&D stage of our own production?

So where do we stop? Where does the alien "external" world begin? Not at the skin, this much is sure. Human beings are and always have been technological animals. Ours is a history of shared technological innovation. Sharpened stones and cave paintings show up 80,000 years ago in the archeological record. We are natural by design; we are designed by nature and culture.

Once this basic fact about ourselves is clearly in focus, we are forced to acknowledge that using steroids or other performance-enhancing drugs does not cross a bright line when it comes to personal responsibility. The athlete's reliance on steroids is no different in principle from a reliance on training techniques, newly designed footwear, sunglasses, mitts, nutrition, or the computer-graphic analysis of plays. We are what we do and we are never entirely self-sufficient in determining the scope of what we can do.

18 | WHAT CAN A PERSON DO?

These reflections on drugs, baseball, and the ways medicine and other technologies change us (enhance, extend, scaffold us) invite us to consider, in more general terms, the question of human abilities.

So let's begin with a joke:

When is it the case that you both can and cannot swim?

Answer: When there is no water.

I came up with that by myself.

Okay. Not very funny.

But the joke points to a curious and fascinating fact about abilities. Just because you can't do something doesn't mean you can't do it!

If we could get clear about this we'd take an important step toward understanding what we are and, in particular, understanding how we make ourselves up over and over again.

Let's take a stab at it: abilities are not identical to their exercise. This is why, although you need light to see, you don't go blind every time you switch off the lights. And this is why you can still swim when you are in the desert, even though you can't. Water and light are conditions on the exercise of the ability to swim and see, respectively; they are enabling conditions. But they are

115

not conditions on the possession of the corresponding abilities themselves.

You don't go blind when the lights are smashed. But you do go blind when your eyes are damaged. How come? Well, light is an enabling condition on the exercise of sight, but your eyes are part of the very machinery of sight itself. The ability survives disruption of enabling conditions, but it doesn't survive the destruction of the mechanism. Destroy the engine and you destroy the car's ability to drive; put the car up on a lift and you prevent it from driving without destroying its ability.

So we've got two pairs of distinctions: ability versus exercise, and mechanism versus enabling condition.

This is where things start to get interesting. The second distinction between enabling conditions and mechanisms is important, and it's reasonably clear. But nevertheless, the line between the two isn't (and can't be made) sharp.

To bring this out, suppose you were living in a far-off future where medical technology has made replacing eyes as easy as replacing contact lenses. Hurt your eyes? No problem, just go to the eye doctor and get a newly grown pair. If eyes were as replaceable and as cheap as, well, new light bulbs, it strikes me that it would be pretty natural to think of them the way we think of light and light bulbs—as enablers of the exercise of our ability, rather than as constituents of the ability's underlying mechanism. This doesn't mean that the distinction between a mechanism and an enabler can't be drawn at all. It just means that we need to ask ourselves anew: What governs our judgments about how to draw the line in a given case?

Suppose a champion skier loses her leg in an accident. Does she thereby lose the ability to perform her trademark jump? She can't do the jump. No chance. That's not in doubt. The question is: Has she lost the ability, or is she merely unable to exercise the ability she retains because an enabling condition is unmet (no leg)? Is the loss of the leg like turning out the lights? Or is it like damaging the eyes?

Can we answer a question such as this definitively?

Yes, and no. Yes, because there usually is an answer. No, because there is no one-size-fits-all answer. Remember the old philosopher's quip: for the Martian, it is not the fact that the arsonist struck the match that caused the conflagration; responsibility lies with the fact that the atmosphere is full of oxygen!

And so with mechanisms and their limits. Are the pen and paper I use to solve math problems part of the mechanism of computation itself? Or are they merely enabling conditions on my exercise? This is a bit like the case of oxygen and the match. If we take the ready availability of writing implements (and knowledge of the actually very complicated algorithms for calculating with arithmetical notation) for granted, then it seems reasonable to think of these as background conditions, and we look for the ability to be housed elsewhere.

But if we step back and take up the perspective of the engineer or the evolutionary psychologist, it becomes startlingly clear that our cognitive powers in the domain of arithmetic are driven in part by our mastery of a symbolic tool set. From this perspective, then, it looks like a lot of what a person can do depends on the way he or she is connected to and in dynamic exchange with the environment, including, importantly, the symbolic and technological environment.

The significant point really is not that we can't draw a sharp line between what counts as part of the mechanism and what counts (merely) as a condition enabling the exercise of the mechanism. The point is that we don't want to.

Back to eyes, sight, and light. In a very real sense, light is no longer merely an environmental condition on the exercise of our ability to see. We are like miners with special helmets: we make light and shine it on the world. Looked at this way, artificial light can seem an intimate part of the mechanism whereby we explore the visual world.

Consider architecture. A building provides a system of artificial constraints, both enabling and limiting what you can do. Want to go upstairs? Well, you've got to use the stairs, and the stairs themselves dictate not only what sort of path you'll follow through space but also how you will coordinate your body parts and movements along the way.

The architect bullies and forces you to do things as he or she determines. At the same time, there would be no "upstairs," and so no possible reason for you to go there, if not for the building. So now consider the life you lead in this building; maybe you live there, maybe you work there, maybe you are there to see a doctor or a lawyer. Can we even begin to separate the building as enabler of your ability to conduct your affairs from the building as constituent of those abilities themselves? Well, yes, depending on our interests, we could or might do this. But the critical thing is this: to be an architect is to be in the business precisely of manipulating your know-how or, more positively stated, of affording you new opportunities for reconstituting what you can do. Architecture is in the business of playing with the boundary between the external enabler and the internal mechanism.

Architecture recapitulates what we all do, as individuals, and as a species, in relation to the world around us. The most critical constraint of all is our past action, for our past action shapes the environment we live in like nothing else (cataclysms aside).

So we ourselves author that which constrains us most. As the poet Antonio Machado wrote: "you lay down a path in walking." And having done so, our subsequent course has been set, for the path we ourselves have made now entrains our movements. It is very difficult to leave the beaten path!

What can you do?

19 | IN DEFENSE OF BARRY BONDS

Babe Ruth hit 29 home runs in 1919. This was a new record, and it electrified a baseball world that was still in shock over that year's Black Sox Scandal. In response, baseball's owners decided to introduce a change that would radically alter the game.

Prior to 1920, a single ball was used for the length of an entire game, or for as long as possible. Fans were expected to return foul balls to play. As cricket is still played today, the condition of the ball is a significant factor in the course of play. Skilled pitchers can use the scratches, smudges, and buildup to influence the ball's action and so to befuddle hitters.

What happened in 1920 is this: baseball introduced a new practice of removing balls from play as soon as they acquired the least imperfection. This practice, which continues to the present day, had the effect of substantially shifting the balance of power from pitchers to batters; the clean-ball rule seems alone to have launched the era of the "live ball." Babe Ruth hit 59 home runs the very next season, and then 60 in 1927, a record that stood until Roger Maris hit 61 home runs in 1961.

Baseball traditionalists insist that Maris's record should come with an asterisk, because he managed his feat in a lengthened baseball season. Question: Did Maris achieve less in hitting 61 home runs than Ruth did in hitting 60 because it took him longer to do it?

But wait a second. Does not Ruth's achievement also deserve an asterisk? This much is true: if we want to understand what Ruth accomplished, we need to take into consideration the fact that Ruth, but not an earlier generation of athletes, was playing in the era of the shiny ball. He couldn't have achieved what he did if not for changed circumstances.

Traditionalists take Babe Ruth's accomplishment as baseline, and against this baseline they mark, or put an asterisk next to, Maris's record. But the decision to treat Maris's performance as the *marked case* and Ruth's as *unmarked* is entirely arbitrary.

To appreciate this, consider that we might very well mark *all* pitching achievements prior to the 1969 season with an asterisk. After all, in that season MLB *lowered the pitching mound*. This came in the aftermath of the 1968 season in which Bob Gibson and other pitchers so totally dominated batters that it was felt something needed to be done to raise the level of hitting. The mound was lowered to achieve precisely this outcome.

The biggest change of all to transform baseball was the decision to allow nonwhite players to compete with white players. Was Babe Ruth the best player of his generation, as so many believe? One thing we know for sure: black athletes were prohibited from competing against him, and Ruth was prohibited from testing himself against them. We also know that Ruth's lifetime record of 714 career home runs was eclipsed within a few decades by an African American, Hank Aaron.

Why do we mark Maris's achievement but not that of white players before integration, or pitchers before 1969? There are probably many factors influencing our feelings about the game and its history. But crucially what we are left with, in the end, are just feelings, or prejudices.

Which brings us to the question of Barry Bonds. Bonds towered over baseball during his career. He towered over a generation of players, many of whom, like him, may have used PEDs.

And it is true that admitting that Bonds and others may have used drugs to elevate their performance may make it harder to make meaningful cross-era comparisons of baseball achievement. But as we have been considering, the challenges we face making cross-era comparisons are nothing new. And Bonds's alleged reliance on PEDs is in itself no more a disqualification than Koufax's reliance on the high mound, or Ruth's on segregation and the shiny ball.

The upshot of the fact that conditions of play vary through history—conditions comprising everything from the exclusion of blacks from the Major Leagues to the configuration of the field and the ball itself—is not that we cannot make cross-period comparisons. We can and we should. No, the upshot is that we need to admit, when we are trying to think through these comparisons, that numbers never tell the whole story of a human being's achievement, even in a sport like baseball where statistics are highly refined. There aren't single metrics for understanding human achievement.

Barry Bonds deserves a place in the Hall of Fame, right there beside Babe Ruth and Hank Aaron. Even if he did use steroids.

20 | LEGALIZE IT!

Rocky's coach forbade him to have sex with his girlfriend while he was in training. Was this because he would be so tired out by sex? Or was it that the coach believed it would alter Rocky's drive, or mindset, somehow making him happy and relaxed, depriving him of the agitated drive, the hunger, to win? I was just a kid when I saw the movie. I didn't really understand.

I don't remember our freshman-year track coach telling us anything about honor, spiritual cultivation, or the joys of competition. I do remember him explaining the difference between aerobic and anaerobic exercise, ways to control painful lactic acid buildup, and of course, advice about what and when to eat before a meet.

Both these examples remind us that sports has never been concerned alone with what goes on in the ring, or on the field, but always also with the cultivation of oneself.

All sports are like Formula One. The goal is to win, but the project is to make the optimal vehicle, and then to learn how to use it, and tune it, and transform it—yourself!—into something capable of going beyond the limits of what is possible. And so athletes—or rather, their coaches and teams and cultures—study and experiment.

Biochemistry, nutrition, training regimens, all with an eye to self-transformation. Look at carbo-loading, for example. Swedish scientists back in the 1960s devised an elaborate system for maximizing glycogen levels in the muscles of marathon runners. The idea, roughly, is to run a long race about a week before the marathon, depleting the muscles of their glycogen stores. This is followed by a rest period with a very low carbohydrate diet. By now the muscles are starving for glycogen and are ready to take even larger amounts on board and store it up. Now the runner is ready to binge, eating as much high-carb foods as he or she can in the run-up to the race. This is an ingenious way to combine eating, resting, and running to jigger the body's default biochemistry and so to achieve a biochemical state of readiness for the start of the big race.[1]

From this standpoint, it is natural, appropriate, and entirely in accord with the *spirit* of the project of athletic achievement to explore and then exploit the benefits afforded by new knowledge and new technologies. So-called blood doping—maximizing one's ability effectively to transport oxygen to the muscle fibers by blood transfusions (one's own, or someone else's)—is a brilliant and creative solution, an entirely *natural* next step once you've tapped out other techniques (such as sleeping at high altitudes or in oxygen tents).

Why ban blood doping?

Because it isn't natural!

Nonsense! What is more natural than *blood*?

---

1. For more on this, see Chris Cooper's *Run, Swim, Throw, Cheat: The Science Behind Drugs in Sport* (New York: Oxford University Press, 2012).

Transfusion isn't natural, though. It's medical. Scientific. It's icky. Syringes, hoses, blood. Yuck!

Is it natural to sleep in a tent with low oxygen levels? Or to take a cable car up to sleep and then back down to train?

What does "natural" mean today anyway? What has it ever meant? Transfusion is used widely in our society as a therapy for a wide range of illnesses and complaints. It isn't strange, unheard of, foreign. It's an appropriate means to an end.

The thing is, you will say, the transfusions allow you achieve higher levels of red blood cells than you could through other training means; it allows you to reach higher levels in a shorter period of time.

To which the correct reply should be: Yes! That's the point!

Athletes are clever and they don't give up. They find new ways, new solutions. *That* is the sport.

It is hard to discern any principled difference between blood doping and carbo-loading or high–low altitude training.

And this is why athletes dope. Not because they are vain, or weak-willed, or set on taking what is rightfully someone else's. From their perspective, there is no principled difference between "doping" and legitimate forms of training (beyond the mere fact that doping is proscribed). Their project, after all, is to figure out a way to transform themselves so that they can do it better than anyone else. This is what they do.

The upshot: doping isn't cheating. And that's why, despite the punishments, and despite the bans, athletes keep doping. It isn't just that they fancy they won't get caught. It's that they can't really take seriously, finally, the idea that doping is doing something wrong.

Of course, in a strictly legalistic sense, doping is cheating. If the rules say "no blood doping," then you break the rules if you transfuse.

But there are two points to be made about this.

First, you can't ban every new molecule, synthetic or otherwise, whose ingenious consumption can be shown, in combination with hard work, to improve performance. You can't ban ingenuity. And so you should not blame athletes for coming up with new cocktails that evade the letter of the law. This is what they do. This is how they think.

Second, we have to come back to the underlying question: *Why* should blood doping, or erythropoietin (EPO), or anabolic steroids be banned in the first place? As I have been arguing, I don't believe there is a satisfactory justification for prohibition.

And this has two consequences.

The first is straightforward. Sporting authorities will never win the arms race. They'll always be one step behind the athletes. What they will do is destroy the careers of *some* athletes. They will humiliate them and dishonor them. But for every athlete they injure through disqualification, there are others who will escape detection.

The second consequence is more subtle. The anti-doping authorities will never convince the athletes that they shouldn't try to dope, just as they'll never convince them that it's wrong to think about food, sex, and sleep.

We treat athletes like tax cheats. But really, they are just working the loopholes. As they must. This is what they do.

There are good reasons not to take drugs to enhance athletic performance. It can be very dangerous, for one. But here's a news flash. *Sports are not good for you*. Athletes transform themselves into performance vehicles. Just look at the bodies of the athletes at the Olympics! Natural? No way. Examples of sound mind in a sound body? No way!

One last point. Our prohibitionist attitudes are actually quite new; they are intimately connected to our society's fifty-year-old demonization of drugs, alcohol, cigarettes, and such like. In contrast, the athletes' permissive interest in recipes, cocktails, and regimens for maximizing success is as old as the hills. It is the spirit in which ancient Greek athletes, or warriors, made sacrifice to the gods so that *they* would intercede on the behalf of mortals and so assure their victory. Is that fair? Maybe not. But it isn't "unsportsmanlike."

In the future, I believe, and I hope, we'll look back on the anti-PED hysteria as a strange aberration, a sign of our moral immaturity.

21 | HOW MUCH BASEBALL IS TOO MUCH?

It used to be that if you were a pitcher and you blew out your ulnar collateral ligament—the ligament that holds your elbow together—you were done.

Goodbye, playing days.

That was the verdict that was handed down to Tommy John, then a pitcher for the Los Angeles Dodgers, when his elbow went pop. But he was dogged and lucky and just happened to be under the care of a doctor, Frank Jobe, with a novel idea about how you might take a piece of healthy tendon in the wrist and use it to tie the elbow back together. The body would do the rest, he thought, plastically transforming the tendon, at the cellular level, until it really became a new ligament. If the surgery were to work—what a feat of imagination to believe that it might really work!—you'd have a new elbow.

Start the clock again and launch a new career.

Well, it did work, and Tommy John did launch a new career. Despite having been declared DOA, he was able to go on to pitch fourteen more seasons and, indeed, to do so at the very top level.

Since John underwent that first replacement surgery, the operation has been performed more than 10,000 times. Draw up a short list of contemporary pitching stars. You'll be astounded how many of them have had Tommy John (as the surgery is universally known): Stephen Strasburg, Matt Harvey, Yu Darvish, Jacob deGrom, Jose Fernandez (now deceased), Chris Carpenter, Adam Wainwright, and on and on.

What's going on here?

The null hypothesis is that pitchers have always been blowing out their elbows, never to be heard from again. In the olden days (before 1974), that would have been that. Now, they just need to get their elbows refurbished and they're good to go.

But that can't be right. The thing about Strasburg and Harvey and deGrom and Fernandez and so many of the others is that these guys didn't go under the knife the way John himself did—to extend an otherwise mature career. They had their elbows rebuilt *at the very start* of their careers; they did that so they could *have* a career.

And there's another piece of the puzzle: although at the time they blew out their elbows these pitchers had only just begun to prove themselves at the Major League level, they were one and all hugely hyped and widely regarded, already, as superstars.

Jeff Passan, in his book *The Arm*,[1] takes a hard look at what, in the words of Hall of Fame pitcher John Smoltz—himself a beneficiary of Tommy John surgery, and the first member of the Baseball Hall of Fame "to sport the scar"—is really an "epidemic" not only of elbow injury but also of elbow surgery to remedy the affliction.

---

1. Jeff Passan, *The Arm: Inside the Billion-Dollar Mystery of the Most Valuable Commodity in Sports* (New York: HarperCollins, 2016).

Passan makes a powerful case that the problem's roots lie in youth baseball. Or rather, in a complex set of developments that have changed not only how kids play baseball but, in a way, also childhood itself; these changes have created new "moral hazards" that parents, coaches, and the sport at all its levels are only beginning to fathom.

Passan quotes Smoltz, who felt called upon to address this topic in his Hall of Fame induction speech in 2015:

> It's an epidemic. . . . It's something that is affecting our game. It's something that I thought would cost me my career, but thanks to Dr. James Andrews and all those who came before him, performing surgery with such precision has caused it to be almost a false read, like a Band-Aid you put on your arm. . . . I want to encourage the families and parents that are out there to understand that this is not normal to have surgery at 14 and 15 years old. That you have time. That baseball is not a year-round sport. That you have an opportunity to be athletic and play other sports. (342)

What's going on here? As Passan makes very clear, it's a complicated story. I think it goes something like this: Kids who love baseball *love baseball*, and they want to play. They dream of the big leagues. It used to be that when Little League was over for the season, that was it. You played basketball or football. It also used to be that parents left kids more or less to their own devices while they took care of work, home and hearth.

Well, that's changed. Parents are keener than ever before to get involved with helping their children live out their dreams—or the deferred dreams of their parents, as the case may be—and in recent years there has been a growing bounty of new baseball opportunities, for-profit, pay-as-you-play leagues, that enable parents to do just this.

In a way, these are vanity leagues—you pay to travel and play with other boys whose parents can also afford to participate in tournaments put on by organizations that keep track of how you're doing, build up rankings, perform talent evaluations, and create a whole hugely costly and hugely profitable baseball resort culture. What starts out as pay-to-play recreation, not all that different from traditional, community-based Little League, begins to assume the guise of *the only way forward* if you're serious about baseball, indeed, if you want to have a chance at a college baseball scholarship and, just maybe, a career in baseball. In fact, real MLB scouts attend the tournaments. Poor kids get left out, of course. But ambitious parents do it because they want to give their sons a leg up on fulfilling a dream of a life in professional baseball. It's a vicious circle.

Of course it isn't all bad. What is better than organized opportunities for kids who love baseball to get a chance to develop their talents and cultivate themselves for a shot at success?

But the downside is obvious. Prepubescent boys are pseudo-professionalized at way too young an age; the things of childhood are made objects of stress and unhealthy competition. Boys are made to play too much baseball. They are asked to throw too much and, more and more, thanks in part to the ubiquity of the radar gun as a gauge of precocious talent, to throw harder, and for longer, than ever before. A good thing goes awry: children overuse and abuse their young bodies.

And now we are reaping the consequences. An epidemic of arm surgery on young men in the late teens and early twenties.

Who's at fault here? Not the kids, obviously. The parents? The coaches? Why aren't they protecting their kids?

There's no simple answer here, either.

For one thing, it's hard to recognize the contours of an epidemic if you're an individual stuck inside it.

For another, how can you tell when *your* boy—who seems, after all, to be made of rubber, joy, and pure energy—is hurting himself? We like to pretend that there are experts we can call on to make these judgments. But there are no experts, not really.

I wrote Passan and asked him about this. Here's what he said: "I've struggled with this. What is 'proper' conditioning? Is it cardiovascular? (Bartolo Colon and CC Sabathia say no.) Is it core? Lower-body strength? Flexibility? I don't know the right answer, and accordingly I have trouble adjudicating this one. I mean, it's something of a cop-out to say: Depends on the guy. But I really do believe that's true. Jose Fernandez blew out a few months after he became a hardcore cyclist. Was that causative? Possibly. Or maybe it was his delivery. Or his genetics. All of this is still such a mystery. It makes the pursuit of knowledge simultaneously invigorating and frustrating."

Passan hits the nail on the head. How do you protect yourself when you are, to borrow a phrase, deep inside the tunnel of your own ambition? We need knowledge. But, really, we need wisdom. There are unlikely to be any one-size-fits-all solutions.

There is an additional moral cost that Passan does not focus on in *The Arm*. As a society, we seem to have a totally incoherent set of values regarding the place of medicine and technology in the cultivation of athletic talent. We categorically prohibit the use of strength-building and injury-protecting PEDs, yet we allow surgical interventions like Tommy John to become business-as-usual, letting pitchers use their body well beyond biologically sanctioned safety and performance specs.

What's the principle that differentiates these? Maybe the biggest difference, as Passan suggested when I raised this issue with him in our correspondence, has more to do with "long-held stigmas than anything particularly rational."

Is it right to expect pitchers to undergo surgery so that they may be able compete at the highest level? Is that any more acceptable than demanding that they should take steroids? Is it any safer?

Passan's book provides another piece of the puzzle.

It isn't only the superstars who are getting Tommy Johns. It's players at every rank and level. And the personal costs—the risks of surgery, the hell of rehabilitation, the emotional risks of losing everything, a whole career, to elbow injury—are enormous and very grim. The physical pain and scarring, the suffering, the insecurity, the stress.

Is this what it should cost to have a chance at a life in baseball?

22 | THE ATHLETE AND THE GLADIATOR

If there is value in spectator sports, it has something to do with the opportunities they provide for teaching us about human striving, doing, the surmounting of obstacles and the very many different ways there are of failing to make it over them. Sometimes we are beaten and sometimes we beat ourselves; luck is often the decider. And sometimes we make our own fate.

Let us return once again to the crucial question: Why are we—fans of all stripes—so offended by the use of performance-enhancing drugs in sports? I take it for granted that we are.

The short answer, obviously, is that we view someone who dopes to improve athletic performance as a cheater. But again, let us ask, *why*?

I have been urging that this is not merely because they violate the rules or the law. No, it would be cheating to take drugs, I think we feel, even if the specific medicines (molecules) in question were not banned. It was cheating before anything was banned. That's why we banned it.

Our thinking is vague here. I have been proposing that it goes like this: doping improves performance in ways, we somehow feel, that athletes can't take credit for. The results improve, but the performance of the athletes does not. Not really. They merely fake it, making it appear as if they can accomplish what in fact they cannot.

Now just why we should think this is true of the use of performance-enhancing drugs has been our question. But let us approach it now by turning to a different piece of the puzzle.

A recent study shows that, while we probably view the athlete who dopes to win as a cheater, we are less likely to condemn as a cheat a student who dopes to improve academic performance.[1]

Why should this be? If, as I have been suggesting in earlier chapters, we reject the use of drugs in sports because they destroy agency, diminish responsibility (praiseworthiness or blameworthiness) for the things we do, then this ought to apply to domains outside of sports. If a kid's success in the math class depends on his taking a med, then shouldn't we say that it isn't really his success at all?

We need to look for what differentiates these cases elsewhere. Here's a proposal: academic study aims at knowledge, and knowledge, we are inclined to think, is a good in itself. If you can solve differential equations, or read books in foreign languages, then that's good, and it doesn't really matter how you got there. In effect, you can't really cheat at learning. Shortcuts are just that—shortcuts!

But not so with sports. When it comes to sports, ends and means collapse into each other; method and result are one. It's not crossing the finishing line first that counts; it's *winning*. But you

---

1. T. Dodge, K. J. Williams, M. Marzel, and R. Turrisi, "Judging Cheaters: Is Substance Misuse Viewed Similarly in the Athletic and Academic Domains?" *Psychology of Addictive Behaviors* 26, no. 3 (2012): 678–682.

win only if you play by the rules. In sports, the goal is only valuable in the context of the game. It isn't just that the cheater doesn't legitimately win. The cheater does not even legitimately play.

But there's a fly in the ointment. The suggestion that the goals in sports—faster, higher, stronger, and so on—are only valuable in the context of the fair play of the game is untenable. Winning has rewards that are concrete and entirely extrinsic to fair play. We shower winners with love, glory, and celebrity, not to mention million-dollar endorsements.

We wouldn't blame a gladiator for juicing. After all, what's at stake in the arena is survival itself, and the value of survival is absolute. But we look the other way when it comes to the gladiatorial reality of our present-day sports industry. What good is fair play to the losers, to the ones who don't bring home medals? To those whose careers end in injury? To the ones who never show up on the Wheaties box or on morning television? Their losses are real and are not confined to the playing field.

It's hard to get athletes to speak frankly about this, but I suspect that this is really how they, as a community, see things. This would certainly explain the fact that the history of sports over the last thirty years or so makes it pretty clear not only that athletes cheat, that they will cheat when they can get away with it, but also that they will find new ways to cheat when the old ways no longer work.

They cheat because everything they know and hope to achieve depends on victory, and there is literally nothing to gain from losing.

They cheat because, if I am right, they don't experience themselves as cheating at all. Like the gladiator, or the scholar, they are simply doing what they need to do to survive.

Baseball Memories

23 | HEARTBREAK AND SOCIAL MEDIA

It wasn't a baseball drama but, rather, a life drama that was on display during a televised Mets–Padres night game at Citi Field in New York on July 29, 2015. It was us and our reliance on, and misplaced confidence in, Twitter and other new technologies of would-be connectedness that were put on the spot.

Rumors swirled on Twitter and in the blogosphere that the Mets had agreed to trade utility infielder Wilmer Flores and young right-handed pitcher Zack Wheeler to Milwaukee in exchange for Brewers star centerfielder, and former Met, Carlos Gomez. Wheeler was on the disabled list (DL) that night, but Flores was on the field at shortstop.

Mets announcers Keith Hernandez and Gary Cohen wondered aloud why Flores hadn't been pulled from the game already; it was their understanding that all that was holding up the trade were medical checks. Why were the Mets running the risk of Wilmer Flores's getting hurt in that evening's play? The internet had confirmed the deal: the Wikipedia page on Gomez listed him as a New York Met and the *New York Times*, *Sports Illustrated*, and ESPN noted the trade as a done deal. I know because I checked.

Eventually, word of the trade reached Flores on the field; he later explained that it was fans shouting from the stands who told him he'd been traded. Terry Collins, the Mets manager and the oldest manager then serving in Major League Baseball—and maybe, it was now revealed, perhaps its least connected to social media—hadn't heard anything about a deal.

Anyway, Flores did finally learn about it and he did so in front of an audience of 30,000 and under the glare of broadcast television. Cameras zoomed in on him as he wept openly on the field. It was like *The Truman Show*, with tight shots of the sniffles and slow-motion replay of him wiping away his tears.

Flores is from Venezuela originally. He'd been drafted by the Mets when he was sixteen. These Mets were his teammates. He'd known no other team. They were dumping him—getting rid of him for someone better. He was being sent away. They hadn't even told him to his face. There, in front of the whole world, he was crying.

It was painful to watch, a new, ultra-brutal kind of reality TV. My son leaned into me on the sofa. Keith and Gary were outraged: I heard them speak of the ill-use of Flores on display; he was being put in an untenable situation. Why in the world was he playing?

I guess you do need to be a baseball fan, and a Mets fan at that, to appreciate the backstory on all this.

The Mets of 2006—young superstars David Wright and Jose Reyes, as well as Carlos Beltran and Carlos Delgado, and others like Cliff Floyd—had been serious postseason contenders. It was a time of great promise and excitement for the team. The following year, however, after coming into the season's home stretch with a dominant seven-game lead over their division rivals, they lost twelve of their final seventeen games and were eliminated from postseason play on the final day of the season.

The same thing happened all over again in 2008; I was one of the many fans who could only weep with disappointment when the Mets, on the very last day of the season—and against the same team that had eliminated them the year before, the Marlins—lost again.

For the Mets of 2015, it has been a long, slow rebuild. The details needn't concern us here; suffice it to say that it didn't help the Mets' reconstruction effort that that the team's ownership had lost very heavily in the Bernie Madoff affair. It's been really hard to be a Mets fan.

But things were starting to look up. The Mets had recently put together a stable of young pitchers that was the envy of Major League Baseball, and even though their offense has been historically ineffective, with key players on the DL, the team was in second place and had a fighting chance of making the postseason.

This is the setting in which the news of the trade for Carlos Gomez was received—two days before the trade deadline. Flores, if truth be told, has been widely criticized for his unsatisfactory play at shortstop, and Gomez was a big bat—maybe just the sort of difference-maker that the Mets needed.

So, even as Mets fans felt for Flores as he broke down on the field, and even as the fans heaped scorn on the Mets management for doing this to him under the glare of the lights, it was also a time of celebration and euphoria. The arrival of Gomez, together with other promotions and acquisitions, would put the Mets over the hump and in serious contention for a pennant. And in a way, the mistreatment of Flores seemed almost like a ritual act: with the final sacrifice of this young man, the bad years would be behind us and we would set forth on a new beginning.

Like I said, a whole new and very brutal kind of reality TV.

Fast-forward. Immediately after the game, it was announced by Mets General Manager Sandy Alderson that there had been no deal. Flores wasn't going anywhere. Wheeler hadn't been traded. The Mets had not acquired Gomez.

Twitter had jumped the gun. The reporters who had posted on Twitter had jumped the gun. Keith and Gary had jumped the gun. The fans who told Wilmer he was shipping out had jumped the gun.

What really happened? Hard to say. Reports have proved unreliable. Reporters had been tweeting that Alderson backed out of the deal when it became clear that Gomez actually had hip problems. His agent, Scott Boras, flat-out denied that Gomez had ever had any health problems, full stop.

The trade, or failed trade, is not my story, however. The story here is how a heady mix of desire, rumor, and fantasy, powered by instant media, looped its way down not only into the Mets broadcast booth but also all the way to the Mets dugout itself and from there out onto the field—where a young and vulnerable Wilmer Flores was made to live out a social-media lie.

In the old days, media was one thing, the public was another, and the events being reported were a third. But these distinctions have now become blurred. The public, via Twitter, has become the media, and the newsmakers themselves, in this case the players, are media consumers like the rest of us.

There are a few people who must have known what was going on all along. Sandy Alderson, for example. He would have known if there had been a deal and he would have known it was going to fall through because of concerns over the health of Gomez. (Anxiety about Gomez's hip didn't prevent the Astros from jumping in and snagging him the next day.)

But the hero of the story, in a way, is Terry Collins, the Mets manager. He's not plugged in and, as a result, he's out of the loop. At first this made him look like a jerk, putting the traded Flores into play. Then, it made him seem just plain out of it: How could he not be in the know about what was happening? But in the end, we can see that he was above it all. Or, to shift the metaphor, beneath it all.

The announcers and the reporters and the fans and the tweeters can play their game up there in the cloud. The work of baseball happens on the field.

24 | THE MATT HARVEY AFFAIR

When baseball fans in New York think back on memorable events from the 2015 baseball season, there's no doubt that the Matt Harvey Affair is one of the things they'll remember.

Matt Harvey was at that time the ace of the Mets' staff, their star pitcher. He was in his first season back from Tommy John surgery. With a playoff spot in plain view, Harvey's agent, Scott Boras, went public with the announcement that Harvey's doctors didn't want him pitching a full load that season.

The team and the fans felt blindsided. Harvey himself may have been blindsided. He certainly didn't handle frenzied questions from the press very well. In particular, he wouldn't commit to playing for the Mets if they were to make it to the playoffs; he wouldn't commit to doing what was necessary to get the Mets there in the first place. At least at first. Eventually he regrouped, made his own decisions, and came to be a huge part of what made it possible for the Mets to clinch their division that season for the first time in nearly a decade.

But not before the you-know-what hit the proverbial fan. At the height of the furor over Harvey's concern that he would hurt himself, Mike Lupica in the *Daily News* wrote:

Matt Harvey needs to know that if he eventually stops pitching for the Mets this season because of an arbitrary innings limit in his first season back from Tommy John surgery, then he will be remembered around here, for as long as he pitches around here, as the star Mets pitcher who quit on his team because that's what his agent told him to do.[1]

Now, there are three things to be said about this.

First, it's a gorgeous sentence.

Second, it's bonkers. As Mike Powell argued convincingly a bit later in the *New York Times*,[2] Harvey had been nothing but gritty, hard-working, and determined in his comeback from elbow ligament reconstruction. And he'd been pitching *very* well. Harvey had been a key element in the Mets' success all season long.

If he were going to have a future in baseball, with the Mets or anyone else, he had to protect his arm. That meant taking the advice of his surgeon. It's worth stressing that there's little evidence that the Mets had ever been tempted to overuse him; he was rarely asked to throw more than 100 pitches in a game all season long. And the Mets introduced a six-man rotation for stretches to give him rest. Plus, they had had him skip a start or two so he could rest.

Third, however bonkers Lupica's sentiments may be, millions of New Yorkers, including me (I admit), felt exactly this way. How could a healthy player opt to sit on the sidelines because maybe,

---

1. Mike Lupica, "Matt Harvey Will Be Remembered as the Mets Ace Who Quit If He Stops Pitching Because of Innings Limit," *Daily News,* September 5, 2015.

2. Mike Powell, "Best Move for Matt Harvey: Shield Arm, and Ears," *New York Times*, September 6, 2015.

possibly, he could get hurt if he were to play? Where's the gladiator in Matt Harvey? Where's the Dark Knight, as he was then known, our very own Avenger? How could he put his own interests before those of his team?

Many of us felt shaken, upset—*angry*—by the thought that Harvey might not be willing to pitch going forward.

But I write today as a philosopher, not as a diehard Mets fan. The striking thing is that this isn't yesterday's news. As I write now, Matt Harvey's career has floundered. He has not managed, till now anyway, to make a complete comeback from a later injury and is fighting not so much for his former glory as the Mets ace, as — having been traded unceremoniously to the Cincinnati Reds — to keep his job in the Major Leagues. At the time he was traded, it was clear that he had never really been forgiven by Mets fans. The feelings of injury and disappointment that were stirred up during this whole brouhaha hadn't been forgotten. And that certainly informs how people are responding to Harvey's current dire straits.

And my question, a philosophical question, really, is *why?*

It's inappropriate to respond to a kid the way you would to a grown-up. Knowing that the person who stepped on your toes is a kid diminishes any irritation you might feel. The knowledge affects, or at least it should affect, how you feel.

But why doesn't the knowledge that Harvey only said what everybody already knows—that his interests and that of the team may not always coincide, that he's got doctors to give him medical advice and agents to give him professional advice, and that he can't simply ignore that advice however much he might want to—assuage our sense of injury?

It isn't news that teams do not make always decisions based on what's good for a player. And, similarly, everyone knows, in the era of free agency, that players have only a minimal loyalty to their teams. But if we know all this, then how could the mere fact that Harvey was open about needing to at least consider the recommendations of his doctor and agent have produced such angst?

Granted, one piece in all this is that *we* are just selfish. The playoffs were in reach, and we all thought we needed Harvey to get there; the thought that he might not be available filled us with horror.

But that does nothing to explain the enduring feeling of injury. That doesn't explain my own sense of, *Oh, no, say it ain't so!*

There must be some deeper explanation.

Perhaps we can find a clue in the pages of James P. Carse's book, *Finite and Infinite Games.*[3] Carse noticed that it is a feature of games that, as he put it, we play them freely. This means that we are free to stop playing anytime we want.

But it's also the case, he writes, that it frequently does not seem to us as if we are free to stop. We get caught up in the games we play. We frequently take our play very seriously. And, indeed, taking the game seriously, getting caught up, feeling compelled to struggle to win is, to some degree, necessary for success. You couldn't excel if you didn't give yourself over to the game, if you didn't care.

If Carse is right, then success in games and sports requires something like a self-lie. Games aren't really important, at least not

---

3. James P. Carse, *Finite and Infinite Games: A Vision of Life as Play and Possibility* (New York: Free Press, 1986).

in themselves, and nothing compels us to play them, or to watch them. But to play them really well, or to follow them as a fan, you need to act as though they matter, as though they compel attention and demand action. We enjoy freedom, but we act somehow under the self-deceiving guise of necessity.

Maybe this is the key to understanding how it is that Harvey managed to break so many sports-loving hearts. He didn't tell New Yorkers or show New Yorkers anything they didn't already know. That's just the point. He reminded them of what they know perfectly well, but choose to forget.

He reminded them—or, rather, he reminded *us*—of what we have to pretend we don't know if we are going to take sports as seriously as we do. For example, he reminded us that his own health is more important than whether the Mets win or lose, that he is merely an employee of the team, that his interests and those of the team are not one and the same, that he's got a financial interest in his health—an interest that would, more likely than not, one day lead him to leave New York and play for another team.

This should not surprise. This is unveiling what we ourselves hide from view. These are truths we willfully ignore.

25 | EXPLAINING THE MAGIC OF THE BALLPARK

No doubt some of the autograph seekers leaning across the fence straining for the baseball players' attention were in it for the money.

I suppose a baseball signed by the right person is worth something. Others were collectors working to complete their sets.

But most of us clumped up along the side of the dugout were fans—and our motives were of an entirely different nature.

Well, to be accurate, I wasn't begging for autographs. My kids were. I was there as a chaperone.

But I'd be lying if I pretended that I didn't feel the same jittery delight that my kids experienced when the players sauntered over to talk to us and sign hats and balls.

After the Mets defeated the A's in Oakland, Mets third baseman David Wright strode up to where my kids were standing near the dugout, and he tossed them his batting gloves and wristband.

How can I begin to describe the joy and excitement that rained down upon us? Let us sing the song of David! Let us count his excellences! Let us rejoice in the blessing!

Those of you who are not fans may snigger. But that, finally, brings me to my question: What is this thing called fandom?

What is it that motivates the fan to meet players or get their autographs? What explains that distinct, inextinguishable magic of the ballpark?

I think I get the cynical line on all this. We had spent a fair bit of money on tickets to manage to be in a spot where David could flip us his branded merchandise. And, for all I know, his action may have been scripted by the manufacturers, or by MLB, or by his own PR staff. Seems like good business. Our continued loyalty as customers has been assured.

But maybe David's action stemmed from something more like love—for the game and for the larger community of people who love the game. *Love* is a good word to use to describe how we feel toward David Wright.

There are things in life that are very hard to understand. The mentality of a fan may be one of those things. Even people who work in sports sometimes get it wrong.

Not too long ago, Kevin Burkhardt, who at the time was an on-air personality for the Mets baseball network SportsNet New York (SNY), tweeted angrily: "Why do guys jump in front of kids to catch a ball thrown over by a player? Even if you give it to the kid, you ruined the thrill you idiot."

Ouch.

Burkhardt's tweet prompted a Twitter outpouring of scorn for guys who kill the thrill for kids.

But Burkhardt and his co-tweeters got it wrong. The reason guys jump in front of kids to catch balls meant for the kids is that, well, when it comes to baseball, they are still kids.

Sure, if you're Burkhardt, or some other professional who works on the other side of the fence, the stadium loses its magic.

But for most people who were baseball fans as kids, the spell has never been broken. The magic is still there. And a trip to the ballpark is a kind of regression. You don't ruin the thrill for the kids by leaping for the ball. You participate in it.

And then you remember yourself. And give the kid his ball.

It is just this childish spirit, unshackled by adult scruples but armed with credit cards—that pays for everything at the ballpark, including Burkhardt's salary.

But we still need an explanation, or even just a better description, of that distinctive attitude of interest and longing, of pleasant anticipation, that marks us when we are fans.

26 | FOR THE LOVE OF THE GAME: PLAY BALL!

For some not inconsiderable portion of the population, life reorganizes itself each spring with the start of the baseball season. Until now, my role in the baseball ecosystem has been clear. I am a fan. I watch baseball, and I think about it. A lot. My ex-wife once referred to herself in my presence as a "baseball widow." I don't really think that was fair. But it is true I don't miss a game the Mets play, time zones be damned. And it is true that love has a lot to do with it. Love of the game, yes. But really: love of my team.

But a few years back, everything changed for me and became exciting in totally new ways. That was when my two boys began playing Little League. Many of you will know what this means. But frankly, I did not.

The best thing I can compare it to is organized religion. Each team is a congregation built around a practice: the play of baseball. Baseball is so complicated, and so big, that it presents itself as task and theory and catechism and phenomenon—a great big question; and all of us try to comprehend it, but stand firm in our commitment even when we can't understand it in truth.

The practice is organized around rabbi- or priest-like figures, the managers or coaches, and their assistants, almost all men, who have the authority to teach and whose ability to teach gives them the authority to talk to our children, and indeed, to us parents, with a sort of straightforward, honest *interest*; they push, hug, drill, and criticize our kids. Watch a uniformed 6-foot giant bending at the waist so that he can place his hand on a 4-foot-tall pitcher's cheek, look him in the eyes, and offer him words that will get him through the inning. It will change the way you see conferences on the mound in Major League Baseball.

The baseball congregation, which is joined to other congregations in a division, which in turn is organized across ages into leagues, is founded, as a church must be founded, on love. Love is the abiding emotion on display in this regimented world of baseball play. The parents are there to love their boys and girls. But you must, and find that you do, love all the children, even the opposing players, and also the coaches, who organize everything, and the folks (us) who groom the fields and bring the snacks and keep score and train the umpires. It is a commitment on everyone's part.

Some of the kids are naturals. For some it's a real test. As with school, or with Sunday school. And for the parents, well, think about it. Practices and games, all over the place. Your kid can't play unless you are there, committed, car keys in hand, willing to get them where they need to be when they need to be there.

It takes a loving community to make organized baseball possible, and baseball itself becomes a kind of monument to community itself, a sort of standing lesson in what a community is and can be.

I myself did not grow up in this sort of community. I was part of no church. I did not go to public schools. I never even dreamed of Little League. I lived in Greenwich Village at a time when Greenwich Village prided itself as a place of freedom from precisely this sort of community. I realize now that my love of baseball—my fan's love of professional baseball—was at least in part the expression of a longing for this sweet and joyous sense of common pursuit. Listening to the Mets under the covers on an AM transistor radio was the closest I ever got to the mainstream. To a certain kind of community. (No surprise, then, that it was not possible for me and my kind to abide that white-bread pinnacle of the establishment, the New York Yankees.)

It's spring. Play ball!

27 | HOW TO BE A FAN

My son didn't weep when his beloved 49ers lost to the Seahawks in the 2014 National Football Conference (NFC) championship. His team may have been vanquished, but at least there was ground for hope that the Broncos would stop the enemy from winning the Super Bowl.

Ah, the ways of love and hate in the world of the fan!

When I learned that the British philosopher David Papineau would be teaching in New York City over the next few years, and that he was interested in sports, I knew an intervention would be required. It would be wrong, wouldn't it, to stand by and do nothing to try to warn him against the poisonous lures and dark charms of that powerful baseball empire in the Bronx? So I sent him a letter, and I laid things out as plainly as I could. Light is better than darkness, good is better than evil, and all decent, right-thinking, progressive people in New York are followers of the Mets, and so on and so forth. He replied, quite correctly, that whether or not what I say is true, you don't choose what team to support for reasons, not even good reasons. Choosing a team, as he put it, isn't like buying a washing machine.

Now Papineau has written on this topic at his new sports and philosophy blog, *More Important Than That: How Philosophy Can Illuminate Sport and Vice Versa.*[1]

If you don't become a fan for reasons, he wonders, then isn't it irrational to be a fan? Wouldn't it be better to admire sporting achievement for its own intrinsic qualities, unbiased by partisan loyalties and affiliations?

This is a good question. We can sharpen it: professional sports franchises are capitalist enterprises; these days they use public tax dollars to build stadiums, but set ticket prices so high the average taxpayers can't afford to attend; they buy and sell our beloved players as if they were commodities; the ties that bind them to our communities are weak—they don't hesitate to move out of city centers to more affluent suburbs or even, from time to time, leave town altogether for new markets in other states.[2]

And yet we love them.

That is the right word, isn't it?

We stand by our team. We care about it. We are attached to it. We suffer when the team fails and we rejoice in its victory. We don't abandon our team when it is down, and however frustrated we may be with the team's actions, with management, or with the poor play of our side, we don't for one second think that these are reasons to move our affections elsewhere. And when another team is better, richer, stronger, that gives us no motivation to switch loyalties; it only makes us resent the enemy more.

---

1. Papineau's blog is at www.davidpapineau.co.uk/blog.

2. I recommend Dave Zirin's writings in *The Nation* and in his numerous books for insightful analysis of the politics and economics of professional sports.

Detached admiration for sporting achievement? Not on your life.

Papineau thinks that our devotion to a team isn't quite *ir*rational in the end. He writes:

> Humans are distinguished by their ambitions. Where other animals live in the moment, we humans give meaning to our lives by adopting long-term goals and working to achieve them. We care about our families, countries, villages, schools, reputations, careers, houses and gardens. Some of these are individual projects, while others are collective. But what they have in common is that they create agent-relative values. Once you have made something your goal, it comes to have a special importance for you, but not for those who lack it, in a way it didn't before. So it is with supporting a team. Once you become a fan, the success of the team becomes one of your projects—and to that extent, I would say, there is nothing irrational in your partisanship.[3]

I'm not sure I quite get Papineau's reasoning here. Sure, once you become a fan, the success of the team becomes one of your projects. But that can't be what makes it rational to be a fan. That would get it backwards. Granted, if I am committed to this team,

---

3. From "Why supporting a team isn't like choosing a washing machine," by David Papineau. This article was originally published on his blog, *More Important Than That* (http://www.davidpapineau.co.uk/blog). Some of these ideas were also incorporated into his book *Knowing the Score: What Sports Can Teach Us About Philosophy (And What Philosophy Can Teach Us About Sports)* (New York: Basic Books, 2017).

then it is understandable why I shed tears when they lose. But why should I be committed in that way? Why should I make this my project?

Or perhaps his idea is rather just this: it is our nature to form attachments of this kind, and once we do, they organize our lives. We don't choose which team to love any more than we choose what person to love, or what kind of person we ourselves are. We need to give up the hyper-rationalistic demand that we justify ourselves and our commitments.

I like the sound of this. But I'm not sure. Blind love, like blind patriotism, is a dangerous thing. And, of course, loves are not invulnerable. Sometimes betrayal—a storied case is the Dodgers' move from Brooklyn to LA in 1958—terminates the attachment that joins us to our partners or teams.

And so, it seems to me that, although we don't choose our loves for reasons, we are condemned at last to admit that, our loves are not beyond reason or indifferent to critical evaluation. We are not off the hook. We can't just take our projects for granted.

I think my son's strength in the face of the 49ers' loss displayed exemplary moderation.

28 | MIND OVER MATTER

The legendary Liverpool manager Bill Shankly said: "Football is not a matter of life and death. It's much more important than that."

Philosopher David Papineau quotes these words admiringly in his intelligent and very personal book on sport, titled *Knowing the Score: What Sports Can Teach Us About Philosophy (And What Philosophy Can Teach Us About Sports)*.[1]

This is not a book on the philosophy of sport as much as it is a collection of meditations by a philosopher who happens to be a sports nut. (It has this in common with *this* book.)

Papineau explores questions like: What is choking? How does it differ from other ways in which the performance of the most accomplished athletes can break down (such as *the yips*)? How do players make decisions, and how do teams—groups of individuals who are more than the sum of their parts—force us to rethink decision theory and game theory? He even ventures into terrain that has almost nothing to do with sport, such as the status of race as a category and whether the fact that race doesn't correspond

---

1. David Papineau, *Knowing the Score: What Sports Can Teach Us About Philosophy (And What Philosophy Can Teach Us About Sports)* (New York: Basic Books, 2017).

to anything biologically real gives us a reason to stop using racial categories.

The book is not a treatise; it is more like a recording of conversations the author might be imagined to have had with his buddies after a good game of tennis on a Saturday morning. *Philosophy* is surely not a sport, not on Papineau's definition, or anyone else's. In my view, it is more like an art. But it must be admitted that many philosophers practice it as if it were something sportlike: an activity aiming at the cultivation and exercise not of physical but, rather, of distinctively intellectual skills, and for their own sake. But this is not true of Papineau. His book is motivated by love of sport and by real curiosity about it.

But there is an argument that unfolds here, nonetheless, something like a defense of Shankly's quote. According to Papineau, sports aren't really good for anything: they aren't useful; they serve no purpose. For example, sports aren't valuable because they are diversions from life and all its demands that can be praised or, as Papineau considers, criticized, for just this fact. Sports belong *to* life and are about as intrinsically meaningful, or meaningless, as just about anything else we do, which is to say either not at all, in an ultimate sense, or a whole heck of a lot. We love playing sports, writes Papineau, simply because sports is a setting in which to cultivate our skills and physical capacities and because, as a matter of fact, it is joyous and daunting and thrilling and difficult to do that.

I agree with Papineau that if sports are valuable, it is not because they point to some further good—health? perfection? enlightenment?—that they can enable us to obtain.

But I'm not convinced that the source of the importance of sports in our lives comes down to the sort of experiences of sporting activity had by individual players that Papineau seems to have in mind. Sports are just too social, for one thing. So much of playing sports consists in playing with others for its pleasures and values to be thought of individualistically. To love sports isn't just to love running all those miles alone on a weekend morning, or even the thrill of trying, finally, to manage a new trick in real play with friends. The sporting life is also a life of reflection on sports—and these reflections are social, collective, and communicative.

Which is the second point. Sports are not only social, they are reflective. They are too intellectual to be characterized, as Papineau does, in terms of the individual cultivation of skills and physical capacities.

Now Papineau certainly appreciates the mental side of sports. One of the best bits of his book is his exploration of the ways in which successful sporting performance is a mental—as well as a physical—achievement. In developing this, he rejects, as I do, the idea that physical accomplishment can be divorced from the possession and exercise of powers of concentration and appreciation. A baseball player, a tennis player, a cricket player—they need to use their minds to govern the more distinctively physical aspects of their performances. Papineau rejects, and I agree with him, what he calls the "yoga conception," according to which success at sports requires the achievement of a kind of Zen state of mindless flow and automaticity. No, being good at a sport may mean that you don't need to—indeed, that you shouldn't—focus on the low-level mechanics of what you're doing. But it doesn't mean that you don't need to concentrate, pay attention, and in general, use your head in the right kind of way.

But there is another aspect to the thoughtfulness of sports that this leaves out; there is another way in which the mind gets into the act. Sports, for the player as well as the fan, are always embedded in a setting of talk and reflection. Sports aren't just activities bent on the cultivation of physical skills for their own sake; they are little social worlds in which doing is one thing and reflection on what you're doing is another. But both are very much required.

To be a player who didn't participate in any of that would be like being a speaker who had no second-order views on language and how to talk. That would be an unrealistic, and also an impoverished, conception of what it is to be engaged with sports.

I am offering a generalized version of the point I have been striving to make about baseball throughout this book: when it comes to baseball, to learn to play is also to learn to think, not just about the sorts of first-order problems that arise in the playing, but also in a more second-order way about what it is one is doing. This is the true meaning, as I have been arguing, of keeping score.

29 | REFLECTIONS ON THE "BOYS" OF SUMMER

Back in 2015, David Wright, star third baseman for the New York Mets, bungled a fairly routine play in a game against the Atlanta Braves. He fielded a grounder skillfully, but then instead of throwing to first base for the easy out, he spun around and tried, unsuccessfully, to tag the passing runner. It was the wrong choice, but an understandable one. He followed his impulse instead of making the percentage play.

He acted *exactly* like one of the Little Leaguers on the team for which I am a volunteer coach.

It is a cliché that professional baseball is a kids' game played by men, but I've never been so struck as I am now, serving as a coach, by the sense that the young professionals are really just big kids. They struggle, just like the kids, trying to rise to the challenges the game poses. Execution is hard in baseball, sure, but knowing when to execute, what and how, understanding what the situation requires, takes a kind of knowledge that professionals in their twenties still struggle to develop. It isn't surprising that even stars like David Wright make mistakes. And it isn't surprising that on any given day, at least a couple of my ten- and eleven-year-olds sob quietly on the bench, humbled by the game.

Little League baseball, I've already noticed, is a lot like church. It's a grassroots affair, grounded in commitment, nourished by charity and volunteer spirit. It's loving. The games themselves are the tip of a pyramid whose base is a community vested in the value of learning to play the impossibly difficult sport of baseball.

And the love extends to pros like David Wright. Yes, they may be millionaires, mercenaries working for the highest bidder. But, before that—and besides that—they are lovers and students of the game we love. They are our children.

30 | BASEBALL'S GREAT EQUALIZER

If Bugs Bunny had a pitch, it would be the knuckleball. It weaves and bobs, zigs and zags, and acts like it has a mind of its own. Catchers have trouble catching this pitch. It leaves hitters dazed. Even the pitcher can't really say for sure what it's going to do. And that's the idea. It isn't a power pitch. It isn't a control pitch. It is, precisely, an *uncontrol* pitch.

The idea is to throw the ball with as little spin as possible. This lets the play of the air and wind along the ball's seams determine its trajectory. A good knuckleballer doesn't so much place the ball as he acts like a ball whisperer.

Here's the curious thing: no one in baseball sets out to be a knuckleballer. By and large, it is a pitch of last resort. You turn to it when all else fails—when the fastball no longer pops and when no one is fooled by the change-up. Certainly this was the case with R. A. Dickey, who won twenty games and the Cy Young Award in 2012 when pitching for the Mets. He may be the only knuckleballer in today's Major Leagues. He turned to the knuckleball— started the long arduous process of learning to throw it—to save a sagging career.

If the knuckleball can be so devilishly effective, why don't more pitchers cultivate it as part of their working arsenal? Or, at the very least, why aren't knuckleball specialists a more everyday part of the game?

The only answer I can come up with is that baseball, like life, isn't rational; things aren't always what they are supposed to be. In the culture of baseball—at least our American baseball culture—the knuckleball just isn't sexy.

But what if a young pitcher, someone still in Little League, did set his, or *her*, sights on this pitch?[1] What if someone devoted a *whole* career to it? This would be an exotic species of baseball flower that may not have ever been seen before.

---

1. Chelsea Baker used the knuckleball so effectively that *Sports Illustrated* questioned whether she, or another woman like her, might be able to take mastery of the pitch all the way to a career in professional baseball. In the end, she enjoyed a successful high school career. See Howard Medgal, "Chelsea Baker Dreams of Pitching in College and the Major Leagues. Can She Do It?" *Sports Illustrated,* February 17, 2015.

31 | BEEP BASEBALL

Sports is a celebration of ability and disability.

Take the case of beep baseball.

Beep baseball, invented in 1964, is a variant of softball or baseball for the blind and visually impaired. Google it. You can watch videos online between American teams and teams from Asia. The National Beep Baseball Association (NBBA) sponsors an annual World Series.

In beep baseball, the ball beeps and the bases buzz. The pitcher and the catcher are usually sighted, and they work *with* the batter, who is blind, to provide a pitch he or she can hit. Four strikes and you're out; you're allowed to let one ball pass. Some hitters and pitchers use the passed ball to organize their timing so as to know when to swing on the next pitch.

Pitchers in beep ball want their batters to hit, so the higher the earned run average, the better—and a good pitcher is key to a good *offense*.

There are two bases, each 100 feet away, corresponding roughly to the familiar first- and third-base lines. Which one you run to depends on which one buzzes after you make contact with the ball. You hit, you listen, you run. Blind batters run as fast as they can, unseeing, down the baseline, toward the bases, which are tall foam structures that they need to touch.

The hardest job in beep baseball, according to the experts, is fielding. A sighted spotter, playing for the defense, shouts out a number corresponding to the region of the field to which the ball is hit, to give the fielders some orientation. The defense loses a run if the spotters say anything more than that. The fielder's job is to find the ball and take possession of it before the runner reaches the base. If they do, the runner is out. If they don't, a run scores. (Fielders don't need to throw the ball to anyone to make an out.)

I just wrote that beep is baseball for the blind. But really, as my description makes abundantly clear, it is a game to be played by the blind and the sighted *cooperatively*. Crucially, every team has a sighted pitcher and catcher, as well as a sighted person capable of skillfully performing the role of spotter. As you can tell by watching, it's a tough game in which the blind and the sighted play hard.

One of the very cool things about beep baseball is that it requires silence. So the culture around beep ball is more like Wimbledon 1950 than like anything we see in public sporting events these days. The batters and fielders need to hear the balls and the bases, as well as the spotters and the pitcher. Passing school buses or a rowdy fan can make play impossible. Beep ball is a game of quiet concentration, as well as explosive effort.

Another striking aspect is that this is a sport in which people who can't see are enabled to run and dive and slide and race. The courage this takes is impressive. And the fun is palpable. I suspect that a good portion of the fun in playing beep baseball comes from the pleasure in trusting others to protect you and support unrestrained movement.

Playing beep baseball at a high level is not only good fun, it's obviously also an impressive sporting achievement. The NBBA World Series gives us an opportunity to think anew about human ability and disability.

32 | BASEBALL MEMORIES

I was on the mound, the game was in later innings, and the Italian kids were trailing. I say "mound," but we played on concrete. Word must have gone out that the Italians were losing, because the fence was crowding with older brothers and friends; they stared menacingly as they leaned into the metal wire. They were not there to watch but, instead, to enforce a victory, or to punish us for ours. My team's captain, Buddy, replaced me as pitcher. I took over at first. That's where I was when the Italians rushed the field. I ran. We all ran. At the corner, I looked back along MacDougal Street and watched a group of three or four older boys close in on Buddy. They'd gotten his shoes off and were slapping his face with them. I kept running.

The Flyers were not a gang. We were a softball team. We had shirts to prove it. Freddy had organized the shirts at a shop on 14th Street, where his mom had connections. The lettering on his shirt didn't come out right. Now Freddy *was* a bit of a gangster. He had the walk; hand on crotch, sort of limping. And I had seen him hanging out with some seriously bad people like Piggy and the Go Club. And he was older and bigger. But I wasn't afraid of him and I wouldn't let him have my shirt. I still have it. The Flyers. Green shirt. White arms. Number 7.

We weren't a gang, and I wasn't tough—a word with a very definite meaning to anyone who grows up in the city—but I remember once walking down the street with the Flyers, in a group, spread out, bats in hand, owning the sidewalk and feeling as though we were somehow menacing.

But we weren't part of a league, either. We would meet at the park on Houston and Sixth, or in Washington Square. Or sometimes at the big field on Mercer, where they were planning to build the NYU gym. We practiced. We hung out. And every now and then, we faced off against kids from a different neighborhood. This was strictly a kids' operation. I don't remember many of the boys that well. There was Tiggy. And there was Buddy, who was older than me and had a blond crew cut, and was tall and skinny and always wore faded white V-neck T-shirts and knee-length shorts. I did once go over to Buddy's place. It was a ground-floor apartment behind a bar on Sixth Avenue next to the Waverly Theater. I remember you had to go through the bar to get to it; it was light outside but very dark in there. His father was sleeping on the couch, even though it was the middle of the day.

The Italian kids were big trouble, though. They were dangerous. They menaced the neighborhood. You couldn't walk past the church at the corner of Bleecker and Carmine without getting assaulted. *Jew! Faggot!* They shouted abuse as they tried to run you down.

My mom's shop was open all day till late, and when I was little the Italian boys from around the corner would come over. They would break our toys. Later on, we set up target practice with rocks and bottles in the empty lot at the corner of Third and LaGuardia.

Sally, Mikey, Frankie, and the others tore off when I accidentally hit my brother in the face and knocked some teeth out.

Once I watched the older Italian boys encircle a bum in Washington Square Park. He was black and he was standing near a burning garbage can to keep warm. They pushed him around and around, and then took his uncooked chicken in the paper Grand Union bag and tossed it into the fire. Even as they beat on him, he tried to save his food from getting ruined.

I wasn't nearly as street smart as I should have been, considering how much time I spent out on the streets. I used to hang out below Shona's window. I was not much older than nine or ten, but I was devoted to her and I was content to spend hours in front of her house, tossing a rubber ball against the wall, hoping she'd look out and see me. I used to talk with the delivery boy at Ottomanelli's butcher shop. One day, I don't know why, but I think it must have been to impress Shona, who was watching from above, I threw a water balloon at him as he sat on his delivery bike, with the big metal compartment up front for holding meat. He was angry and gave chase. He was a young man, dressed in a white butcher's coat. "Stop thief!" he shouted as he ran after me. An old lady clawed at my arm. I ripped myself free and ducked down into an underground parking lot on Jones Street. That's where he caught me.

There was one Italian girl I liked. I remember her from that playground on Sullivan Street. She was much older. She might have been called Angela. She was gangly and tall, and looking back, I'm pretty sure she would not be considered pretty. But I liked her, even though I don't think I ever spoke to her. But we knew each other by sight. She'd ride the swings, reading a fan magazine. On the other side of the fence, tall boys with switch blades teased her.

"David-faggoty fan!" they sang. I was a David Cassidy fan. Maybe that's what drew me to her.

One day, the Flyers climbed into the locked field on Mercer Street. We were just about to start practice when we saw the Italians flooding over the fence at the far end of the field. They were still out to punish us. We climbed the fence and took off.

These are my first baseball memories, set against the backdrop of a Greenwich Village that no longer exists and that is on its way to being forgotten. It is striking to me, as I think back, how baseball for me, like childhood, was largely an adult-free zone, and that it was always joined with danger. It was one long showdown. With thugs. With other boys. But it was also a showdown with the game itself. With its challenge not just to execute and deliver but also to be responsible and to look one's self, and others, in the eye.

ACKNOWLEDGMENTS

When I was a boy, we had an old tube radio. It was a huge wooden box, and it took what seemed like forever to warm up. I would sit next to it, bent over, following the baseball game with intense focus. Because we were in the country, reception was spotty at best; I'd miss whole plays and had a hard time keeping track of what was going on. But in my memory even the static, not to mention the soft tones of my team's announcers, the occasional crack of the bat, and the jarring loud beer commercials, was a joy to take in.

This must be a trick of time. I suspect that if my memory were more accurate, what I'd really recall is the intense frustration that we didn't have a better radio. Or a TV! It's not that we were poor, Depression-era folks living in the country, even though that was definitely a Depression-era radio. No, I was raised in Greenwich Village in the 1970s, and spending late summer in Upstate New York was, I suppose, for my parents, a way of getting away from TV. And anyway, they were not baseball folks. They were artists. Baseball had about as much connection to them, and to our New York City life, as 4-H clubs and Republican politics.

Which is maybe why I loved it so, and why I loved and still love—with a passion that I sometimes find hard to make sense of—the New York Mets. I was too young to travel out to Flushing by myself to see them play. The Mets lived, for me and for my brother, over the rainbow, in a dreamy world of static and late-night radio magic.

Fast-forward: these days I am a philosopher and cognitive scientist at the University of California at Berkeley. I don't get out to see the Mets play that often, but I have the internet package, so I get to watch every game, from wherever I happen to be. A lot has changed in the time it takes to grow up. The world is different. The Mets are different. The game itself has changed. And I've changed too, and I've at least tried to learn a thing or two about baseball, about life, and given my work, about the human mind and the nature of consciousness.

Infinite Baseball is a book about baseball; it's not a book about me, but it is a book about why baseball is worth loving. Really, it's a book about why baseball matters, and why it has much to teach even those of us who aren't lifetime devotees of the game.

In *Infinite Baseball* I argue that baseball is a game, one might almost say, *about* agency and responsibility. To think about baseball is to think about human beings and the limits of our agency—not the limits of what we can do but, rather, the limits of what we can take credit for. I don't mean that baseball is an instructive object of comparison for philosophers and scientists interested in such questions. I mean that baseball itself really is a philosophical game in the sense that it demands of any one who enters the baseball world—whether as fan, as professional athlete, or even as Sunday softball player—that he or she participate in the distinctive thinking practice that defines the game. If I am right in this, baseball has much to teach us about values, the law, the nature of language, and the origins of writing, action, freedom, and, yes, the meaning of life.

Or you could say that *Infinite Baseball* is an apology or a defense. It's my answer to those—like my father, or ex-wife, or friends outside the United States—who might ask: Why baseball? Why care about that?

A number of people helped me learn to love baseball. Jerry Berg, my back-door neighbor, was the closest thing I ever had to a baseball mentor. We played catch across the street on the lawn in front of the First National City Bank; one summer day he came to the park where I was with my team, the Flyers, and he surprised me with a spontaneous invitation to join him for an afternoon at Shea Stadium. Jerry explained the infield-fly rule to me and introduced me to many of baseball's finer points.

My mother was not a baseball fan as such, but she was open to it insofar as she was interested in life's dramas in whatever form they might take. She got the game, and even more, she appreciated how much it meant to me. We like to sit together even now watching the Mets on TV.

My brother Sasha is a hockey fan first, but our shared love of the Mets is, for me, one of life's sweetest things.

And then there is my son Ulysses, who is the player I never became and whose baseball knowledge now outstrips my own.

I would like, also, to mention Tiggy Eldred. He lived on MacDougal Street and was one of the kids I played softball with. His confident play made a big impression on me. I am pretty sure that it was his mom who got my mom to bring me down to the park one Saturday morning so that I could join the team. Tiggy probably doesn't remember me.

Adam Franks invited me to join National Public Radio's science and culture blog *13.7: Cosmos and Culture* in 2010. At that time, in addition to Adam, who is an astrophysicist, the other regular contributors to *13.7* were the physicist Marcelo Gleiser, who had co-founded the blog with Adam, and the biologists Stuart Kauffman and Ursula Goodenough. Our editor at NPR, in many ways our leader and certainly our biggest supporter, was Wright Bryan. I remember telling Adam during that first phone conversation that if I signed on, I wouldn't want to be confined to writing about cognitive science and philosophy, although these are obviously my home fields. I specifically mentioned baseball as a topic I might want to write about. This book almost certainly wouldn't have come to be if Adam had not warmly supported this suggestion. I am grateful to him, to Wright, and the others, for the opportunity to be part of the *13.7* community. Thanks also to later additions to *13.7*: anthropologist Barbara King, psychologist Tania Lombrozo, and also Meghan Sullivan, who took over editorial duty after Wright's departure and who did so much to develop the blog.

About a decade ago I had separate conversations about baseball with Hans Ulrich Gumbrecht and Stephen Metcalf; it occurs to me now that I've had them in mind as imagined baseball interlocutors ever since. I am grateful for this inspiration.

Thanks to Russell Weinberger, at Brockman Inc., for his early encouragement for this project; to John Protevi, and also my mother Judy, for careful, critical comments on earlier drafts, as well as to Nick Merrill and Thi Nguyen for helpful advice. Thanks to Lawrence Weschler, not only for introducing me to the Robert Francis poem which serves as the epigraph for the introductory essay, but also for reminding me, by his own example, how good it is possible for writing to be. Thanks to Paul Holdengräber, of the New York Public Library, for pointing me to the quote from Kierkegaard that serves as this book's epigraph.

I am grateful to these students and friends at Berkeley, members of my Friday Group: Caitlin Dolan, Samantha Matherne, Bengt Molander, B. Rousse, Marjan Sharifi, David Suarez, and Joseph Kassman-Tod. I am grateful to others for more indirect support and inspiration: to Christopher M. Hutton, whose work on language has enabled me to appreciate the connections with baseball that I explore here; to Edward Harcourt, for enlightening discussion about baseball and cricket; to Nicole Peisl and Ana Noë, for so much support; to August Noë, for many joyful hours spent watching and playing baseball; and to my father, for his curiosity about the game, and for his abiding skepticism.

A special thanks to Peter Ohlin of Oxford University Press, for shepherding this book into existence.

A note on sources and permissions:
The introductory essay, as well as chapters 18 and 32, were written for this book. All other chapters are reworking of writing originally published on NPR's *13.7: Cosmos and Culture* website (www.npr.org/13.7). "Pitcher" is reprinted from *The Orb Weaver* by Robert Francis (Wesleyan University Press, 1960) and is published here with permission of the publisher.

BIBLIOGRAPHY

Angell, Roger. *The Summer Game*. New York: Viking Press, 1972.

Araton, Harvey. "Who Scores Games by Hand Anymore?" *New York Times*, July 11, 2013.

Brandom, Robert. *Making It Explicit: Reasoning, Representing and Discursive Commitment*. Cambridge, MA: Harvard University Press, 1994.

Carnap, Rudolf, Hans Hahn, and Otto Neurath. *Wissenschaftliche Weltauffassung—Der Wiener Kreis*. Vienna: Wolf, 1929.

Carse, James P. *Finite and Infinite Games: A Vision of Life as Play and Possibility*. New York: Free Press, 1986.

Chase, W. G., and H. A. Simon. "Perception in Chess." *Cognitive Psychology* 4 (1973): 55–81.

Clark, Andy. *Natural-Born Cyborgs: Minds, Technologies and the Future of Human Intelligence*. New York: Oxford University Press, 2004.

Cooper, Chris. *Run, Swim, Throw, Cheat: The Science Behind Drugs in Sport*. New York: Oxford University Press, 2012.

Dingemanse, Mark, Nick Enfield, et al. "Universal Principles in the Repair of Communication Problems." *PLOS One*, September 16, 2015. https://doi.org/10.1371/journal.pone.0136100.

Dingemanse, M., F. Torreira, and N. J. Enfield. "Is 'Huh?' a Universal Word? Conversational Infrastructure and the Convergent Evolution of Linguistic Items." *PLOS One*, November 8, 2013. https://doi.org/10.1371/journal.pone.0078273.

Dodge, T., K. J. Williams, M. Marzel, and R. Turrisi. "Judging Cheaters: Is Substance Misuse Viewed Similarly in the Athletic and Academic Domains?" *Psychology of Addictive Behaviors* 26, no. 3 (2012): 678–682. doi: 10.1037/a0027872.

Enfield, Nick. *How We Talk: The Inner Workings of Conversation.* New York: Basic Books, 2017.

Epstein, David. *The Sports Gene: Inside the Science of Extraordinary Athletic Performance.* New York: Current/Penguin Group, 2014.

Gould, Stephen Jay. *Triumph and Tragedy in Mudville: A Lifelong Passion for Baseball.* New York: Norton, 2003.

Harbach, Chad. *The Art of Fielding.* New York: Little, Brown, 2011.

Hernandez, Keith, and Mike Bryan. *Pure Baseball: Pitch by Pitch for the Advanced Fan.* New York: HarperCollins, 1994.

Homer. *The Odyssey.* Translated by Emily Wilson. New York: Norton, 2018.

Law, Keith. *Smart Baseball: The Story Behind the Old Stats That Are Ruining the Game, the New Ones That Are Running It, and the* Right *tWay to Think About Baseball.* New York: HarperCollins, 2017.

Lewis, David. "Scorekeeping in a Language Game." *Journal of Philosophical Logic* 8, no. 3 (1979): 339–359.

Lewis, Michael. *Moneyball: The Art of Winning an Unfair Game.* New York: Norton, 2004.

Lupica, Mike. "Matt Harvey Will Be Remembered as the Mets Ace Who Quit If He Stops Pitching Because of Innings Limit." *Daily News,* September 9, 2015.

Massaro, D. W. "Speech Perception," in James D. Wright (editor-in-chief), *International Encyclopedia of the Social & Behavioral Sciences, 2nd edition,* Vol 23. Oxford: Elsevier. pp. 235–242.

Noë, Alva. *Out of Our Heads: Why You Are Not Your Brain and Other Lessons from the Biology of Consciousness.* New York: Farrar, Straus and Giroux, 2009.

Noë, Alva. *Strange Tools: Art and Human Nature.* New York: Farrar, Straus and Giroux, 2015.

Noë, Alva. "The Writerly Attitude." In *Symbolic Articulation: Image, Word, and Body Between Action and Schema,* edited by Sabine Marienberg, 73–88. Boston: Walter de Gruyter, 2017.

Oates, Joyce Carol. *On Boxing.* New York: Dolphin/Doubleday, 1987.

Papineau, David. *Knowing the Score: What Sports Can Teach Us About Philosophy (And What Philosophy Can Teach Us About Sports)*. New York: Basic Books, 2017.

Passan, Jeff. *The Arm: Inside the Billion-Dollar Mystery of the Most Valuable Commodity in Sports*. New York: HarperCollins, 2016.

Powell, Mike. "Best Move for Matt Harvey: Shield Arm, and Ears." *New York Times*, September 6, 2015.

Putnam, Hilary. *Reason, Truth and History*. Cambridge: Cambridge University Press, 1981.

Schonbrun, Zack. "How Do Athletes' Brains Control Their Movements?" *New York Times*, April 13, 2018.

Schonbrun, Zack. *Performance Cortex: How Neuroscience Is Redefining Athletic Genius*. New York: E.P. Dutton, 2018.

Schwartz, Alan. *The Numbers Game: Baseball's Lifelong Fascination with Statistics*. New York: St. Martin's, 2004.

Starkes, Janet L., and K. Anders Ericsson. *Expert Performance in Sports: Advances in Research on Sports Expertise*. Windsor, Ontario: Human Kinetics, 2003.

Updike, John. *Hub Fans Bid Kid Adieu: John Updike on Ted Williams*. New York: Library of America, 2010.

Will, George F. *Men at Work: The Craft of Baseball*. New York: Macmillan, 1990.

INDEX

Aaron, Hank, 121
ability
  in beep baseball, 167–69
  doping as cheating, 134–36
  exercise versus, 115–16
  understanding, 115–19
academic cheating, 135–36
accountability, 55–56
Alderson, Sandy, 142, 143
Anti-Realism, 93–95
apportioning praise and blame,
  51–53, 55–56
architecture, 118–19
arguing about sports, 37–38
Armstrong, Lance, 107
Arm, The (Passan), 129–31, 133
art museums, 34
at-bat, 33, 86–88
attention, shared, 45–47
autographs of players, 149–51

Baker, Chelsea, 166n1
ballpark, magic of, 149–51
balls
  catching during games, 150–51
  clean-ball rule, 120
  fastballs, 18–20, 18n8
  knuckleballs, 165–66, 166n1
baseball analytics, 15

baseball-like practices, 73–75
baseball memories, 170–73
batters
  apportioning praise and
    blame, 51–52
  check-swing strike, 21
  perception of, 89–92
  runs batted in, 15
  task during at-bat, 86
batting average, 15, 64
Beltran, Carlos, 140
beep baseball, 167–69
blame, apportioning, 7, 51–53,
  55–56
blind and visually impaired persons,
  baseball for, 167–69
blood doping, 124–27
Bochy, Bruce, 39
Bonds, Barry, 111–12, 122
Boras, Scott, 142, 144
boredom
  enjoying slow pace, 36–38
  shortening length of
    games, 31–35
boxing, 12–13, 14n7
box score, 14
Brandom, Robert, 95n1
Braun, Ryan, 99
Burkhardt, Kevin, 150–51

Cain, Matt, 54
carbo-loading, 124
Carse, James P., 8, 147–48
catching balls, 150–51
Chase, William, 90
cheating in academic versus athletic
        domains, 135–36
check-swing strike, 21
chess, 8, 8n6, 90
childhood
    baseball memories, 170–73
    Little League, 33, 152–54, 163–64
    pressure on young players, 131–32
choreography, dance, 45–46
church, Little League compared to, 152–54
Clark, Andy, 106
clean-ball rule, 120
Cohen, Gary, 139, 140
Collins, Terry, 140, 143
Colon, Bartolo, 132
communication
    coordination in, 46–47
    game of, 85–88
    language as baseball-like
        practice, 71–78
    linguistic universals, 79–84
    perception in, 89–92
communication technology, 106
community, behind youth baseball,
        25, 153
control of players, 33–34
convergent evolution, 83
conversation
    game of, 85–88
    linguistic universals, 79–84
    perception in, 89–92
Crawford, Brandon, 40

cricket, 120
cross-era comparisons, 120–22
cyborg-nature of human being, 105–7

dance choreography, 45–46
danger in sports
    common injuries, 109, 110
    elbow injuries, 128–33
    Matt Harvey affair, 144–48
Darling, Ron, 21
Degrom, Jacob, 64n2
Delgado, Carlos, 140
Dickey, R. A., 165
digestion, 73
Dingemanse, Mark, 79–84
distributed decision-making, 33
doping
    academic cheating versus, 135–36
    by Barry Bonds, 122
    blood, 124–27
    as cheating, 134–36
    cyborg-nature of human being, 105–7
    drug specialist supervision of, 110
    justification for prohibition, 126–27
    as plagiarism, 109–14
    surgery versus, 99–104
    3-D imaging for training
        versus, 108–14
drug specialists, 110

earned run average (ERA), 14–15
earned runs, 7–15, 52
economics of sports, 156
elbow injuries
    Matt Harvey affair, 144–48
    Tommy John surgery,
        99–101, 128–33

emotional involvement in
    sports, 147–48
enabling condition versus
    mechanism, 115–19
Enfield, Nick, 79–84
evolution, convergent, 83
exercise versus ability, 115–16
experts versus novices, 90

fans
    autographs of players, 149–51
    choice of team to support, 155–58
    joint attention of, 45–47
    magic of ballpark, 149–51
    passion for sports, 144–48
    selfishness of, 144–48
fastballs, 18–20, 18n8
favorite teams, choice of, 155–58
fielding, in beep baseball, 168
Fernandez, Jose, 132
Finch, Jennie, 91–92
Finite and Infinite Games
    (Carse), 147–48
finite games, 8
Flores, Wilmer, 139–43
flow, myth of, 10–11, 161
Flyers, 170–73
forensic concepts, 7n4
forensic sport, baseball as, 51–53, 103
foul/strike rule, 31
Francis, Robert, 1, 20, 87, 92

Galarraga, Armando, 96
galloping horses, 108
game of communication, 85–88
Gibson, Bob, 31, 121
gladiators, 134–36

Goebbels, Heiner, 45–46
Gomez, Carlos, 139–43
Gooden, Doc, 54
Gould, Stephen Jay, 2–4

Harvey, Matt, 45, 144–48
hearing speech, 74
Hernandez, Keith, 86n2, 139, 140
hits
    apportioning praise and blame, 51
    determination of, 66
Holtzman, Kenny, 57
Homer, 27–28
home runs, as practical structure, 74
horses, galloping, 108
Hosmer, Eric, 39
"Huh?" as universal word, 81–84
human abilities, 113–14, 115–19

importance of sports, 147–48, 160–61
infinite game, 8, 9
instant replay, 39–41, 93
intellectual writing about
    baseball, 2–5
Internal Realism, 94–96
    in the zone, 10–11

Jobe, Frank, 99–101, 128
John, Tommy, 128
joint attention, 45–47
Joyce, James, 96

Kansas City Royals, 39
keeping score, 59–62
kids
    baseball memories, 170–73
    magic of ballpark, 149–51

pressure on young players, 131–32
professionals compared to, 163–64
Knowing the Score: What Sports Can Teach Us About Philosophy (And What Philosophy Can Teach Us About Sports) (Papineau), 159–61
knowledge-making activity, keeping score as, 61
knuckleballs, 165–66, 166n1
Koufax, Sandy, 19, 31, 99

language
    baseball compared to, 72–78
    communication game, 85–88
    complexity of, 6, 6n3
    learning, 74–75
    linguistic competence, 75–76
    linguistic universals, 79–84
    Paradox of Speech, 71
    perception in, 89–92
    relation to writing, 76–78
Law, Keith, 63–67
legalization of blood doping, 124–27
length of game
    enjoying slow pace, 36–38
    shortening, 31–35
Levinson, Jerrold, 5
Lewis, Michael, 15, 65
life, baseball as imitation of, 3, 12
linguistic competence, 75–76
linguistic universals, 79–84
Little League, 33, 152–54, 163–64
live-ball era, 32
live games
    magic of ballpark, 149–51
    versus televised, 42–44
Lock, John, 7n4

love of the game
    choice of team to support, 155–58
    Little League, 152–54
    magic of ballpark, 149–51
loyalty to teams, 155–58
Lupica, Mike, 144–46

Machado, Antonio, 119
magic of ballpark, 149–51
Maris, Roger, 120–22
Massaro, D. W., 72n1. *See also* language
math problems, solving, 117–18
meaning of life, 54
mechanism versus enabling condition, 115–19
medicine. *See also* Tommy John surgery
    Barry Bonds use of steroids, 122
    blood doping, 124–27
    carbo-loading, 124
    cyborg-nature of human being, 105–7
    doping as plagiarism, 109–14
    drugs versus surgery, 99–104
    human abilities, 115–19
Meija, Jenrry, 102
memories of baseball, 170–73
mental side of sports, 161–62
miscommunication
    communication game, 85–88
    perception and, 89–92
    repairing, 79–84
Moneyball (Lewis), 15, 65
Monnier, Matthilde, 45–46
motion-capture technologies, 108–14
myth of flow, 10–11, 161

national pasttime, 25–26
natural-born cyborgs, 106
New York Mets
    Carlos Beltran, 140
    Carlos Delgado, 140
    David Wright, 140, 149–50, 163–64
    Jenrry Meija, 102
    Johan Santana, 54
    Jose Reyes, 140
    Keith Hernandez, 86n2, 139, 140
    Matt Harvey, 45, 144–48
    Mike Piazza, 91
    R. A. Dickey, 165
    spectator reaction in Game 7 of
        2015 World Series, 45
    Tom Seaver, 54
    Wilmer Flores, 139–43
    Zack Wheeler, 139
New York Times, 31, 60, 139
no-hitters, 54, 55–58
normative forensic structure, 12–13
novices versus experts, 90
numbers
    baseball analytics, 15
    box score, 13–14
    controversy over use of, 13–18
    earned run average, 14–15
    importance of, 16–18
    new methods of statistical
        analysis, 63–67
    pitcher wins, 15–16
    runs batted in, 15–16
Numbers Game, The (Schwarz), 15, 65

Oakland A's stadium, 38
Oates, Joyce Carol, 12–13n7
official scorekeeper, 61, 66

on-base percentage, 15
outs, determination of, 66

Panik, Joe, 39, 40
Papineau, David, 155–56,
    157, 159–61
Paradox of Speech, 71
Passan, Jeff, 129–31, 132–33
passion for sports, 147–48
perception in communication, 89–92
perfect games, 54, 56–58
performance-enhancing drugs (PEDs)
    Barry Bonds use of, 122
    as cheating, 134–36
    cyborg-nature of human
        being, 105–7
    justification for prohibition, 126–27
    as plagiarism, 109–14
    versus surgery, 99–104
persons, as forensic concept, 6–8n4
philosophical game, 5
phronesis, 10
Piazza, Mike, 91
pitchcast, 21
pitcher-batter relationship,
    18–20, 33–34
pitchers
    apportioning praise and blame, 52
    earned run average, 14–15
    evaluation of performance by, 64–65
    fastballs, 18–20, 18n8
    knuckleballs, 165–66, 166n1
    Matt Harvey affair, 144–48
    no-hitters, 54, 55–58
    perception of, 89–92
    perfect games, 54, 56–58
    task during at-bat, 87

Tommy John surgery,
    99–104, 128–33
    wins, 15–16
Pitcher, The (Francis), 1, 20
pitching mound, lowering of, 121
plagiarized performance, 108–14
Plato, 1, 71
play-by-play announcers, 43
playing ball
    beep baseball, 167–69
    Little League, 152–54
    reasons for, 160–61
play reviews, 39–41
popularity of baseball, 3–4, 25–26
Powell, Mike, 145
practice, baseball as, 9–10
praise, apportioning, 7, 51–53, 55–56
pressure in youth baseball, 131–32
Pullum, Geoffrey, 89
Pujols, Albert, 91
Putnam, Hilary, 95n1. *See also*
    Internal Realism

quantitative analysis, 63–67

racial segregation in baseball, 121
Rattle, Sir Simon, 45, 46
Realism, 93–95
Reason, Truth and History (Putnam),
    95n1. *See also* Internal Realism
reflective activity, baseball as,
    5, 161–62
reflective looping structure, 12
religion, Little League compared
    to, 152–54
Reyes, Jose, 140

rules of baseball, 31–32, 72–73
runs, apportioning praise and blame
    for, 52
runs batted in (RBIs), 15, 64, 66
Ruth, Babe, 32, 111, 120–22
Ryan, Nolan, 19, 54

Sabathia, CC, 132

sacrifice hits, 7
San Francisco Giants, 39, 54
Santana, Johan, 54
Schonbrun, Zack, 18n8
Schwartz, Alan, 14, 65, 108n1
scientific disciplines, development
    of, 22–23
scorekeeping
    apportioning praise and blame,
        7, 51–53
    official scorekeeper, 61, 66
    personally keeping score, 59–62
    writing story down, 12–14
Seaver, Tom, 54
segregation in baseball, 121
self-deception, 147–48
selfishness of fans, 144–48
Selig, Bud, 36, 37
Shankly, Bill, 159
shared attention, 45–47
Simon, Herbert, 90
Six-Million Dollar man, The, 105
slowing down, 37
slow-motion replay, 39–41
slugging percentage, 15
Smart Baseball (Law), 63–67
Smith, Linda B., 42

soccer, 37–38

social media, rumors about Flores trade on, 139–43

social worlds, 9

spectators. *See also* fans
joint attention of, 45–47
live versus televised games, 42–44
magic of ballpark, 149–51

speed of game, 21
enjoying slow pace, 36–38
play reviews, 39–41
shortening length of games, 31–35

sports, arguing about, 37–38

Starkes, Janet, 90

statcast, 21

statistics
baseball analytics, 15
box score, 14
controversy over use of, 13–18
earned run average, 14–15
importance of, 16–18
new methods of statistical analysis, 63–67
pitcher wins, 17
runs batted in, 17, 64, 66

steroids. *See* doping

story of game, writing, 12–14

strike zone, 21

Stroud, Barry, 6n3

surgery on pitchers, 99–104, 128–33

Surrogate Cities, 45–46

survival, doping as strategy of, 134–36

talking. *See* conversation

teams, choosing favorite, 155–58

technology
cyborg-nature of human being, 105–7, 113–14
instant replay, 39–41, 93
televised baseball, 23, 42–44
3-D imaging used in training, 108–14

Tommy John surgery
doping versus, 99–104
epidemic of, 128–33
Frank Jobe, 99–101
Matt Harvey affair, 144–48

tools, use of, 105–7, 113–14

training athletes with 3-D imaging, 108–14

transfusions, blood, 124–27

TV, watching baseball on, 23, 42–44

Twitter, 139–43

ulnar collateral ligament (UCL) reconstruction, 99–104
epidemic of, 128–33
Frank Jobe, 99–101
Matt Harvey affair, 144–48

umpires
as judges, 21
play reviews, 39–41
theories of umpiring, 93–96

unearned runs, 52

universals, linguistic, 79–84

value of sports, 147–48, 160–61

vanity leagues, 131

watching baseball
joint attention, 45–47
live versus televised, 42–44

Wheeler, Zack, 139
winning, importance to athletes, 136
wins, evaluation of pitching
        performance by, 64
Wright, David, 140, 149–50, 163, 164
writing
    about baseball, 2–5
    relation to language, 76–78

youth baseball
    community behind, 25, 153
    epidemic of elbow surgery, 130–33
    Little League, 152–54, 163–64
    understanding pace of
        game, 33–34

zone, in the, 10–11